A RIGHT
ROYAL
CHRISTMAS

'The Christmas Tree' by Winslow Homer, from *Harper's Weekly*, 25 December 1858.

A RIGHT
ROYAL
CHRISTMAS

COMPILED BY
HUGH DOUGLAS

McConville

SUTTON PUBLISHING

First published in 2001 by
Sutton Publishing Limited · Phoenix Mill
Thrupp · Stroud · Gloucestershire GL5 2BU

British Library Cataloguing in Publication Data
A catalogue record for this book is available from the British Library

ISBN 0 7509 2791 7

Typeset in 11/16.5pt Sabon.
Typesetting and origination by
Sutton Publishing Limited.
Printed and bound in England by
J.H. Haynes & Co. Ltd, Sparkford.

Contents

An illustration from *The Fir Tree* by Hans Christian Andersen, 1850.

The Compiler's Thanks

I thank all of the contributors, and their publishers, for helping to create this *Right Royal Christmas*. The Royal Archives at Windsor Castle have answered my queries, and permitted me to quote from Royal Insight, the royal website. The University of Virginia Library Electronic Text Center and University of Toronto Department of English and University of Toronto Press have allowed me to use extracts from their websites, and Bridget Ann Henisch has shared her deep knowledge of Christmas customs. My thanks to all of them.

Family, friends, passing acquaintances and even strangers warmed to the task of tracking down royal Christmases over more than a thousand years, and suggested subjects I might well have missed otherwise. Libraries have helped, too, especially the London Library, Peterborough Central Library, York and Brighton Libraries and Williamsport Library in Pennsylvania.

Special personal thanks must go to Betty Adams, Jack and Anne Alster, Caroline Aston, Lynessa Austen, Pat and James Bruce, Clive Burton, Keeta Campbell, Betty Cook, June Counsel, Anne Dewe, Pinny Geffert, Wendy Glavis, Ruth and Pat Haynes, Keith and Maureen Horrox, Helen Litchfield, Hilda and Michael Moorhouse, Ann Phillips, Lin Thomas, and Sir Michael Thomas, who provided ideas, material and pressed books on me in large numbers. As always, my wife, Sheelagh, and members of our family have supported me. To all of them, and with apologies to anyone missed, thank you.

I am grateful to the following websites for permission to quote from them:

www.royalinsight.gov.uk

www.library.utoronto.ca/utel/rp/poems/sggk

www.etext@virginia.edu.

For information on all my books please refer to: http://members.tripod.co.uk/hughdouglas

Every effort has been made to contact owners of copyright of all passages quoted. I apologise for any whom it has proved impossible to trace.

Picture Credits

I am grateful to the following people and sources for permission to reproduce images:

Lynessa Austen, pp. 30, 31, 100; British Library, p. 20; Christ's Church, Williamsport, Pennsylvania, pp. 112, 113; Christmas Archives International, p. 48; Consignia Plc, p. 12; Eastern Counties Newspapers Ltd, p. 6; Viscount de l'Isle's private collection at Penshurst Place, p. 75; Keith Horrox (cartoon reproduced in *The Hogmanay Companion* by Hugh Douglas), p. 79; Hulton Archive, pp. 119, 135; *Illustrated London News*, pp. 93, 96, 106; Pat Marriott (drawing reproduced in *Black Hearts in Battersea* by Joan Aiken), pp. 140–1; Mary Evans Picture Library, p. 17; John Reynolds (from *1066 And All That* by W.C. Sellar and R.J. Yeatman, Methuen Publishing Limited), p. 34; The Royal Archives © 2001 Her Majesty Queen Elizabeth II, p. 101; Royal Pavilion Libraries and Museum, Brighton, p. 89; Sir Michael Thomas Bt, p. 130; D.C. Thomson, p. 42.

The Queen's Christmas

Hugh Douglas and Caroline Aston

Christmas is one of the most precious times of the royal family's year, one of the few occasions when they can enjoy family life together free from public appearances, nagging ministers and official engagements that have to be timed to the minute.

Throughout the centuries kings and queens have traditionally spent the festival at their favourite homes – at Richmond, Sheen, Windsor, Whitehall, Brighton, Buckingham Palace, Osborne House and more recently Sandringham in Norfolk, a favourite royal retreat for the past hundred years. Surrounded by only her closest family, Her Majesty can be her own person there for a few brief days.

So, how does the Queen celebrate Christmas? How different is her day from our own, with its unvaried routine of family greetings, presents and church, followed by a huge dinner of turkey, plum pudding, mince pies and After Eight mints? And afterwards? It is difficult to imagine the Queen settling down in front of the television among the debris of crackers and paper hats to eat more mint chocs and doze off until it is time to watch . . . her very own Christmas broadcast.

Surely the Queen must have something much more royal to do? Not so, thank goodness. By and large the pattern of Her Majesty's Christmas Day follows ours, but with some differences: she enjoys walking and riding, and the exchange of royal gifts takes place on Christmas Eve, leaving her free in the morning to attend an early church service privately. Her 'official' outing to church comes later, when she is photographed. This is the only time the public see her all day – apart from on television, and that is pre-recorded so it can be broadcast at a time appropriate to the global audience it attracts.

The Queen's grandfather King George V and her father George VI used to deliver their message 'live' over the airwaves at 3 o'clock prompt on Christmas afternoon, although when her grandfather's first Christmas message went out live in 1932 broadcasting was not without its hazards. The most unexpected unforeseen circumstance that day had nothing whatever to do with the techniques of broadcasting of the time, however; it occurred when the King fell through the seat of his favourite chair just as he was about to speak.

The royal family's Christmas, like ours, originated from the festival King Alfred wrote into the rights of the people of England more than a thousand years ago, commanding that there should be holidays on Christmas Day and the twelve days following. During that time no free man should be compelled to work. The common man enjoyed this right as best he could while king and courtier spent it in splendid overindulgence, with dancing, gambling and gluttony on a scale that can only be described as 'right royal'.

Despite all the festivities, affairs of state still need to be attended to. There are ministers and courtiers to be dealt with, papers to read and letters to write. So 'minding the shop' has always gone hand in hand with royal merrymaking – ever since a nervous Duke William of Normandy, having slain King Harold a few months earlier, looked over his shoulder warily as the crown of England was placed on his head in Westminster Abbey on Christmas Day 1066. King Henry I, who also ruled over large tracts of France, held his Christmas court more often in Normandy than in England. *The Anglo-Saxon Chronicle* gives some idea of the nomadic life he had to lead to keep his nobles in check: he celebrated Christmas at Westminster, Windsor, St Albans, Brampton, Norwich and Dunstable, and in the year 1111 'bare not his crown' at all at Christmas, Easter or Pentecost. A king's life could be hard.

Murder and mayhem were all too often a part of past royal Christmases. The nomadic, insecure Henry I once cut off the right hands of those who had debased his coinage, and – a macabre touch – chose to do so at Christmastime. Thomas à Becket was put to death by knights acting in the King's name (or so they claimed) on 27 December. Mary Queen of Scots could not resist using Twelfth Night festivities to outdo her rival Elizabeth. Charles I stormed into the House of Commons during the Twelve Days to arrest troublesome members, thus taking a step towards the scaffold and paving the way for Christmas to be banned by the Puritans for a decade.

Compared with the excesses of the Middle Ages, modern festivities are positively tame and the feast frugal. In those distant times Twelfth Night, or Twelfth Day as it was known then, was the highlight, a day spent eating, hunting, gambling and watching mystery plays and masques. On this last day of Christmas, the monarch 'abdicated' and a courtier, chosen by finding a bean hidden in a Twelfth Day cake, became monarch for the day. In Scotland this time of madness was known as the Daft Days.

In the eighteenth century, the House of Hanover introduced innovations such as the Christmas tree from Germany, and these intermingled with tradition to create a very English festival. Prince Albert refined this further until rooms glittered with candle-lit trees, gifts were exchanged and children found stockings filled with presents from Santa Claus awaiting them on Christmas morning. For even the poorest child there was usually at least an orange and a few sweets. The introduction of the Penny Post encouraged people to start sending Christmas cards to distant friends.

Although turkey, that quintessential element in the Christmas feast, only arrived in England in about 1540, within a couple of centuries it had ousted the larks, blackbirds, partridges, quail, doves, swans, thrushes and even the boars' heads and roast beef favoured at earlier banquets. Christmas dinner shrieked of such excess in the early nineteenth century that the gluttonous Prince Regent could not wait to savour his own gargantuan feast. He once held his party below stairs in the state-of-the-art kitchens at the Royal Pavilion in Brighton, where he paid the finest chef in Europe a fortune to cook for him.

The traditional celebration as we know it today may have been largely invented by Queen Victoria and Prince Albert, but they had considerable help from Charles Dickens. Oddly, Dickens never actually mentioned royalty in his Christmas stories, yet he showed his readers all the magical trappings of the season – the illuminated tree, the turkey feast, the presents, the crackers, carols and Christmas cards – which fit so comfortably into this time of joy and goodwill that it is hard to imagine Christmas was ever otherwise.

Thanks to those three – a Queen, a Prince Consort and a 'Prince of Storytellers' – we all enjoy a right royal Christmas today.

What can family, friends and staff expect as a Christmas present from royalty? One Christmas recently the Queen gave each member of her staff – about 2,000 of them – a Christmas pudding from Tesco supermarkets. The puddings must have been easier to carry home than the hunks of bloody meat given in past times, which Caroline Aston describes in her article 'How Different, How Very Different from the Home Life of Our Own Dear Queen', published in the Daily Telegraph *on 23 December 2000.*

George V's tenants were assembled in a freezing coach house to receive a dole of beef. Five bullocks worth of

HM The Queen and the The Queen Mother receiving flowers and gifts from well-wishers at Sandringham, Christmas 2000.

meat was laid out on holly-trimmed trestles and the gory gifts were carried away in white towels.

Queen Mary's friends must have been somewhat unnerved in 1929 when she sent them brocade-covered miniature cupboards, with a helpful note explaining that these were to conceal their telephones in, as she considered phones to be 'instruments of unparalleled vulgarity'. This must be the nearest royalty has ever got to the 'crocheted-crinoline-lady-concealing-spare-loo-roll' school of present, although Queen Elizabeth the Queen Mother (then Queen) raised eyebrows in 1939 when she went Christmas shopping in Aberdeen's Woolworth's.

It's all so much easier these days. All you need to know is that Prince Charles collects lavatory seats and the Queen loves red frocks, crosswords and Billy Bass the Singing Fish.* In fact, today's Royal Family take perverse pleasure in thrift, so it's more likely to be footmuffs than Fabergé.

The Queen and the Princess Royal love nothing more than a good scavenge among the craft fairs and horse shows. Many a royal Christmas stocking has been enlivened by herby hand soap or chunky-knit shooting stockings (quite a change from great-grandpa Edward VII's day when under-endowed beauties used their husbands' shooting hose as falsies to pad out their corsages).

Of course there's always that multitude of shops that are officially designated 'By Royal Appointment'.

Turnbull & Asser in Jermyn Street are purveyors of shirts, ties and dressing-gowns for royal males; over in the Burlington Arcade, N Peal offers a cascade of cashmere twin sets suitable for discerning royal grandmothers. For some years, Princess Diana's sons would always give her a Herond hand-painted china animal, obtained from Asprey & Garrard, while the preferred royal chocolates come from Charbonnel et Walker in Old Bond Street.

The Sultan of Brunei used to send a Fortnum & Mason hamper to Kensington Palace, filled with crystallised fruits, hams, cheeses and biscuits. These days, Prince Andrew and the Earl of Wessex swoon over chocolate Bath Olivers as a teatime nibble, probably after pulling the favoured royal cracker, Tom Smith originals.

---

* A popular toy fish, which moves its head and tail as one walks past it.

Berry Bros & Rudd of St James's Street still produces a perennial favourite nip (the ideal present for cold royal hunters, shooters and fishers) with its The King's Ginger Liqueur. Created in 1905 for Edward VII, when the monarch took to motoring in chilly new-fangled open automobiles, this golden refreshment still appears at many a cold shoot and can be added to Champagne to produce a stunning cocktail.

The possibilities for the royal present hunters are endless and one can always fall back on Price's candles (used on every royal dining-table from Buckingham Palace to Highgrove) or a useful Eximious wash-bag (by appointment to the Prince of Wales, £24.59 – including up to four initials).

The Wise Men

Charles Dickens

In 1849 Charles Dickens wrote The Life of Our Lord *for his own children, explaining to them, 'I am very anxious that you should know something about the History of Jesus Christ. For everybody ought to know about Him. No one ever lived, who was so good, so kind, so gentle, and so sorry for all people who did wrong, or were in any way ill or miserable, as he was.' It was written in his own hand, without publication in mind, and only appeared in print in 1934. Appropriately,*

*it was published in serial form just as his novels had been a century
earlier. Here he relates the story of King Herod and the Wise Men.*

Now the great place of all that country was Jerusalem – just
as London is the great place in England – and at Jerusalem
the King lived, whose name was King Herod. Some wise
men came one day, from a country a long way off in the
East, and said to the King 'We have seen a Star in the Sky,
which teaches us to know that a child is born in Bethlehem
who will live to be a man whom all people will love.' When
King Herod heard this, he was jealous, for he was a wicked
man. But he pretended not to be, and said to the wise men,
'Whereabouts is this child?' And the wise men said 'We don't
know. But we think the Star will show us; for the Star has
been moving on before us, all the way here, and is now
standing still in the sky.' Then Herod asked them to see if the
Star would shew them where the child lived, and ordered
them, if they found the child, to come back to him. So they
went out, and the Star went on, over their heads a little way
before them, until it stopped over the house where the child
was. This was very wonderful, but God ordered it to be so.

When the Star stopped, the wise men went in, and saw
the child with Mary his Mother. They loved him very
much, and gave him some presents. Then they went away.
But they did not go back to King Herod; for they thought
he was jealous, though he had not said so. So they went
away, by night, back into their own country. And an Angel
came, and told Joseph and Mary to take the child into a
Country called Egypt, or Herod would kill him. So they

The first page of Charles Dickens's *Life of Our Lord*, written specially for his own children.

escaped too, in the night – the father, the mother, and the child – and arrived there safely.

But when this cruel Herod found that the wise men did not come back to him, and that he could not, therefore, find out where this child, Jesus Christ, lived, he called his soldiers and captains to him, and told them to go and Kill all the children in his dominions that were not more than two years old. The wicked men did so. The mothers of the children ran up and down the streets with them in their arms trying to save them, and hide them in caves and cellars, but it was of no use. The soldiers with their swords killed all the children they could find. This dreadful murder was called the Murder of the Innocents, because the little children were so innocent.

King Herod hoped that Jesus Christ was one of them, But He was not, as you know, for he had escaped safely into Egypt. And he lived there, with his father and mother, until Bad King Herod died.

Carol of the Three Kings

Robert Graves

The Wise Men were quickly turned into three kings by the Christian Church, and carols have been written about them in many languages. This is Robert Graves's translation of De Drie Koningen (The Three Kings), *an old Flemish carol for Holy Innocents' Day or Epiphany.*

Three Kings are here, both wealthy and wise,
Come riding far over the snow-covered ice;
Royal in throng,
Noble in song,
They search for the Child, the Redeemer of wrong;
With tambour and drums they go sounding along.

The Three Wise Men featured on a postage stamp at Christmas 1982.

God's angel speaks Saint Joseph anigh:
'With Jesus thy charge into far Egypt fly.
Stay not nor stand;
Herod's at hand.'
The ass hastens panting; the hot desert sand
has rescued our saviour from Herod's ill band.

Herod betrays these innocent lives
Both younger and elder to lances and knives.
Who can dare tell
Murder so fell?
These pretty young children in anguish of hell
Were martyred together his anger to quell.

Arthur Rules

University of Virginia Website, University of Toronto Website and *The History and Antiquities of the City of York*, 1785

King Arthur may have lived and ruled in England in about the sixth century AD, or he may be no more than a legend. But he has inspired poets over a hundred generations since the great scholar-poets of the Middle Ages wrote of him, Queen Guinevere, and the exploits of his Knights of the Round Table. Greatest of all the tales of Arthur is Sir Thomas Malory's fifteenth-century Le Morte D'Arthur, *which in turn inspired Lord Tennyson to write his* Idylls of the King *in the nineteenth century. This description of how at Christmas Arthur was chosen king by drawing the sword from the stone comes from the University of Virginia Library Electronic Text Center.*

Then stood the realm in great jeopardy long while, for
    every lord
that was mighty of men made him strong, and many
weened to have been king. Then Merlin went to the
    Archbishop of
Canterbury, and counselled him for to send for all the
lords of the realm, and all the gentlemen of arms, that
    they should to
London come by Christmas, upon pain of cursing; and
for this cause, that Jesus, that was born on that night,
    that he would
of his great mercy show some miracle, as he was come to

be king of mankind, for to show some miracle who
should be rightwise

king of this realm. So the Archbishop, by the advice

of Merlin, sent for all the lords and gentlemen of arms
that they should

come by Christmas even unto London. And many of

them made them clean of their life, that their prayer
might be the more

acceptable unto God. So in the greatest church of

London, whether it were Paul's or not the French book
maketh no mention,

all the estates were long or day in the church for

to pray. And when matins and the first mass was done,
there was seen in

the churchyard, against the high altar, a great stone

four square, like unto a marble stone; and in midst
thereof was like an

anvil of steel a foot on high, and therein stuck a fair

sword naked by the point, and letters there were written
in gold about

the sword that said thus: – Whoso pulleth out this

sword of this stone and anvil, is rightwise king born of
all England . . .

But no knight was able to draw the sword from the stone until
Sir Arthur arrived on New Year's Day.

. . . When he came to the churchyard, Sir

Arthur alighted and tied his horse to the stile, and so he
went to the

tent, and found no knights there, for they were at the
jousting. And so he handled the sword by the handles,
   and lightly and
fiercely pulled it out of the stone . . .

Now,
said Sir Ector to Arthur, I understand ye must be king of
   this land.
Wherefore I, said Arthur, and for what cause? Sir, said
Ector, for God will have it so; for there should never man
   have drawn
out this sword, but he that shall be rightwise king of this
land.

The anonymous Sir Gawain and the Green Knight *brings the
Arthurian legend to Camelot at Christmas again. As King Arthur and
his knights feast at the Round Table a great Green Knight enters,
riding a green horse and carrying a huge axe. He challenges any one
of the knights to strike off his head with a single blow on condition
that in exactly a year's time he will allow the Green Knight to strike
him similarly. Sir Gawain accepts the challenge, and the poem tells of
his travels, adventures, resistance to temptation by beautiful ladies,
eventual surrender to one, and of course his encounter with the Green
Knight at the end of his quest. Sir Gawain has been translated into
modern English by many scholars. This version of the Green Knight's
arrival at Camelot is taken from the University of Toronto Website.*

This King Arthur was at Camelot at Christmas with
   many a lovely
lord, and they were all princely brethren of

the Round Table, and they made rich revel and mirth,
and were free

from care. And betimes these gentle knights

held full many a tournament, and jousted in jolly
fashion, and then

returned they to the court to sing the

Christmas carols. And the feasting was for fifteen days,
and it was

with all the meat and mirth that men could

devise. And glorious to hear was the noisy glee by day
and the

dancing by night, and all was joyous in hall and

chamber, among the lords and ladies as it pleased them,
and they

were the most renowned knights under Christ

and the loveliest ladies that ever lived.

Historians lay claim to Arthur too. He was said to have spent
Christmas in York in AD 521 The author of The History and
Antiquities of the City of York, *published in 1785, accuses him and his*
retinue of overindulging to such a degree that they forgot the true
meaning of the festival. Apparently nothing changes over the centuries!

At this time (anno 521) that great Monarch [Arthur], his
Clergy, all his Nobility and Soldiers, kept his *Christmas* in
York, the first Festival of that Kind ever held in *Britain* . . .
whither resorted to him the prime Persons of the
Neighbourhood, and spent the latter end of *December* in
Mirth, Jollity, Drinking and the Vices that are too often the

Consequence of them; so that the Representations of the old Heathenish Feasts dedicated to *Saturn* were here again revived; but the Number of Days they lasted were doubled, and amongst the wealthier Sort trebled; during which Time they counted it almost a Sin to treat of any serious Matter. Gifts are sent mutually

King Arthur and his knights at the Round Table, from a fourteenth-century manuscript reproduced in Lacroix, *Arts de Moyen Age*, p. 5.

from and to one another; frequent Invitations pass betwixt Friends, and domestic Offenders are not punished. Our Countrymen call this *Jule-tide*, substituting the Name of *Julius Caesar* for that of *Saturn*. The Vulgar are yet persuaded that the Nativity of Christ is then celebrated, but mistakenly; for 'tis plain they imitate the lasciviousness of *Bacchanalians*, rather than the memory of *Christ*, then, as they say, born.

Crowned at Christmas

Simon Schama and John Macleod

At least four times in the past thousand years three monarchs have ruled during a single year: Edward the Confessor, Harold and William I

(Duke William of Normandy) in 1066; Edward IV, Edward V and Richard III in 1483; Edward VI, Lady Jane Grey and Mary I in 1553; and of course George V, Edward VIII and George VI in 1936. Four coronations have taken place at Christmastime: Harold, William I, Stephen and the Scottish coronation of Charles II.

Simon Schama, author of A History of Britain: 3000 BC to AD 1603, *captures the nervous William of Normandy as he was crowned in Westminster Abbey on Christmas Day 1066 when the ceremony ended in panic.*

William knew that no conquest worth its name would be secure without the occupation of London, but instead of tackling the city directly he sent his army around it in a green-belt excursion, perhaps with the aim of starving it into surrender if need be. By the time he crossed the Thames at Wallingford, however, Archbishops Stigand and Aeldred, and Edgar the Atheling were ready to kneel in submission. The last of the Saxon line was now William's hostage, and there was no one left from the old *witan* who could possibly lead any kind of concerted resistance. On Christmas Day 1066, Westminster Abbey saw its third royal ceremony within a year: the coronation of King William I. [The other two were the burial of Edward the Confessor and the coronation of King Harold.] There was an effort to make this a hybrid of Saxon and Norman rites. Read in English by Aeldred of York and in French by Geoffrey, Bishop of Coutances, the rite of Dunstan, which had been created for

King Edgar's coronation at Bath in 973, was enacted but with the addition of a rite used for the kings of France – the anointing with the sacred oil, the chrism. Perhaps this finally made William the Bastard a legitimate king.

It was almost a year since Edward the Confessor had made his deathbed prophecy, and perhaps some of those who had been in attendance in Westminster thought that the many thousands of English dead were atonement enough and that the tree of England might now repair itself and grow green again. But the demons had not quite departed. On his coronation day William had prudently posted knights outside the abbey to deal with anyone who was not demonstrating unconfined joy at the great event. When the guards heard the shouts of acclaim from within, the *vivats*, they concluded that some sort of assault was under way, for which the standard response was to set fire to every building in sight. The historian Orderic Vitalis wrote:

> as the fire spread rapidly through the houses the people who had been rejoicing in the church were thrown into confusion, and a crowd of men and women of every rank and status, compelled by this disaster rushed out of the church. Only the bishops and clergy along with the monks stayed, terrified, in front of the altar and only just managed to complete the consecration rite over the king who was trembling violently. Nearly everyone else ran towards the raging fire, some to fight bravely against the force of the flames, but more

hoping to grab loot for themselves amid such great confusion. The English, believing there was a plot behind something so completely unlooked for, were extremely angry and afterwards held the Normans in suspicion, judging them treacherous.

After this fiasco, it was not surprising that William was not prepared to take the formal acts of homage offered at his coronation at face value. The fort that would become the Tower of London – a stone castle of unprecedented strength – began to be constructed right after Christmas.

The coronation of William I at Westminster Abbey, Christmas Day 1066. This detail is taken from Roy 15 E IV f. 236, Vol. I, by Jean Batard de Wavrin.

The debacle of his coronation was the only time anyone would get a glimpse of William 'pale and trembling'. More often he appeared as the god-like victor: tall – 5 feet 10 inches – red-haired and potent. Around Easter 1067 he felt confident enough to return to Normandy for a triumphal progress through the towns and churches of the duchy. It was an elaborately planned spectacle, with the king departing from Pevensey where he had first set foot on English soil and taking with him, as if the captives of a

Roman triumph, a few tame specimens of the Saxon elite: Edgar the Atheling, and the earls Edwin and Morcar.

On Christmas Day 1651 Charles II was crowned King of Scots, nine years before the monarchy was restored in England following the Civil War and Cromwell's Protectorate. Charles had been living in exile in France and Holland, but in 1650 he returned to Scotland and accepted the National Covenant and Solemn League and Covenant, which for years had come between the Scots Kirk and Stuart kings. In his book Dynasty – the Stuarts 1560–1807 *John Macleod describes the ceremony that took place at Scone, where Scottish monarchs had been anointed since ancient times. The Earl of Argyll arranged the whole affair and he himself set the crown on the King's head.*

Argyll and the Covenanters planned a coronation. It was held at Scone on 1 January 1651, and was almost certainly the last held in Scotland. (There is some evidence that Charles's nephew, the Old Pretender, had a Scots coronation in 1715.) This wintry show at Scone, however, was of unique character. It was a Covenanting coronation and more akin in many respects to the ordination of a Free Presbyterian minister. This sat absurdly, to modern eyes, with the more lavish and sacerdotal elements long associated with coronation rites: but, as an early biographer of Charles remarks, 'a fresh farce was now necessary and His Majesty had a principal part to play in it'.

It was not without pomp. The king was allowed to wear a plush robe of expensive cloth. The sons of noblemen – sound Covenanting noblemen, of course –

were appointed to bear his train. There was a canopy of state, of red velvet, above his throne. But there was no anointing with oil. He received the crown from Argyll and the sceptre from the Earl of Crawford and Balcarres. A leading Malignant was then admitted to the Covenanting fold, in a bizarre ceremony; this John Middleton was garbed in sackcloth. Among other things, Charles had to homologate the Longer and Shorter Catechisms and, of course, the Covenant.

> I, Charles, King of Great Britain, France and Ireland, do assure and declare by my solemn oath, in the presence of Almighty God, the searcher of all hearts, my allowance and approbation of the National Covenant and Solemn League and Covenant above written . . . and I shall observe these in my own practice and family, and shall never make opposition to any of these, nor endeavour any alteration therein.

There followed a sermon of inordinate length by Robert Douglas [a member of the General Assembly of the Kirk]. 'The sins of former kings have made this a tottering crown. . . . A King, when he getteth his Crown on his head, should think at the best, it is but a fading crown.' Afterwards, there was a lavish and no doubt much-appreciated feed. Charles and party partook of meat, partridges, ten calves' heads, and twenty-two salmon. In the days following, as further chunks of Scotland fell to Cromwell's efficient forces, the king made hasty progress about those parts of his realm it was still safe to enter: Pittenweem, St Andrews, Stirling, Perth, Dundee, Aberdeen. He still found time to relax though, and like his forebears, including Mary [Queen of Scots] – and many a Scots tourist since – he enjoyed some time playing golf. . . . He also had a delicate problem with Argyll, who was determined to wed the king to his daughter, Lady Anne Campbell. She must have been of plain appearance: when Argyll, in 1649, met Charles on the Continent with a gift of six Flanders mares, a wag suggested he intended in due time to bestow the Lady Anne as a seventh.

Revenge and Madness

The Anglo-Saxon Chronicle and the Paston Letters

Furious that his coinage was being debased and trade ruined, King Henry I summoned every man who minted money in his kingdom to Winchester at Christmas 1125, and according to The Anglo-Saxon Chronicle *this was the punishment he meted out to them.*

In this year sent the King Henry, before Christmas from Normandy to England, and bade that all the mint-men that were in England should be mutilated in their limbs; that was, that they should lose each of them the right hand, and their testicles beneath. This was because the man that had a pound could not lay out a penny at a market. And the Bishop Roger of Salisbury sent over all England, and bade them all that they should come to Winchester at Christmas. When they came thither, then were they taken one by one, and deprived each of the right hand and the testicles beneath. All this was done within the twelfth-night. And that was all in perfect justice, because they had undone all the land with the great quantity of base coin that they all bought.

Christmas could bring happiness to monarchs too. Henry VI's mind gave way to insanity shortly before the birth of his son Prince Edward on St Edward's Day, 13 October 1453, and for more than a year he was unaware that his Queen had given him an heir. At Christmas 1454 Henry recovered sufficiently to be told of the birth of his heir. Edmund Clere, a member of the royal household, sent the good news to his cousin John Paston. The letter was written from Greenwich on 9 January 1455, and survives among the Paston Letters.

Blessed be God, the king is well amended and hath been since Christmas Day; and on St John's Day [27 December] commanded his almoner to ride to Canterbury with his offering, and commanded the secretary to offer at Saint Edward [Edward the Confessor's tomb at Westminster Abbey]. And in the Monday after noon the Queen came to him, and brought my Lord Prince with her. And then he asked what the Prince's name was, and the queen told him Edward; and then he held up his hands and thanked God thereof. And he said he never knew him till that time, nor wist not what was said to him, nor wist not where he had been while he hath been sick till now.

The Paston Letters: A Selection in Modern Spelling,
edited with an Introduction by Norman Davies, by
permission of Oxford University Press

Murder in the Cathedral

T.S. Eliot

Henry II was troubled by 'turbulent priests', and on 29 December 1170 four of his knights, William de Tracy, Reginald Fitzurse, Hugh de Morville and Richard Brito, murdered the Archbishop of Canterbury, Thomas à Becket, in his own cathedral, believing they were carrying out the King's wish. T.S. Eliot's Murder in the Cathedral *dramatised this moment of murder at Christmas, which shocked all Christendom.*

KNIGHTS
Where is Becket, the traitor to the King?
Where is Becket, the meddling priest?
Come down Daniel to the lions' den
Come down Daniel for the mark of the beast.

Are you washed in the blood of the Lamb?
　Are you marked with the mark of the beast?
Come down Daniel to the lions' den,
　Come down Daniel and join in the feast.

Where is Becket the Cheapside brat?
　Where is Becket the faithless priest?
Come down Daniel to the lions' den,
　Come down Daniel and join in the feast.

THOMAS

It is the just man who
Like a bold lion, should be without fear.
I am here.
No traitor to the King. I am a priest,
A Christian, saved by the blood of Christ,
Ready to suffer with my blood.
This is the sign of the Church always,
The sign of blood. Blood for blood.
His blood given to buy my life,
My blood given to pay for His death,
My death for His death.

FIRST KNIGHT

Absolve all those you have excommunicated.

SECOND KNIGHT

Resign the powers you have arrogated.

THIRD KNIGHT

Restore to the King the money you appropriated.

FIRST KNIGHT

Renew the obedience you have violated.

THOMAS

For my Lord I am now ready to die,
That His Church may have peace and liberty.
Do with me as you will, to your hurt and shame,
But none of my people, in God's name,
Whether layman or clerk, shall you touch.
This I forbid.

KNIGHTS

Traitor! traitor! traitor!

THOMAS

You, Reginald, three times traitor you:
Traitor to me as my temporal vassal,
Traitor to me as your spiritual lord,
Traitor to God in desecrating His Church.

FIRST KNIGHT

No faith do I owe to a renegade,
And what I owe shall now be paid.

THOMAS

Now to Almighty God, to the Blessed Mary ever Virgin,
to the blessed John the Baptist, the holy apostles Peter
and Paul, to the blessed martyr Denys, and to all the
Saints, I commend my cause and that of the Church.

While the KNIGHTS kill him, we hear the CHORUS.

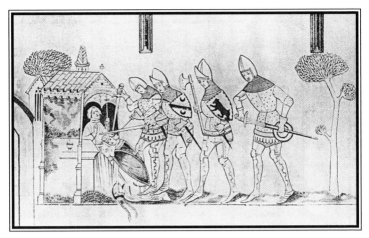

A mural from St Edmund's Church, South Burlingham, Norfolk, depicting the murder of Thomas à Becket.

CHORUS

Clear the air! clean the sky! wash the wind! take stone
  from stone and wash them.

The land is foul, the water is foul, our beasts and our-
  selves defiled with blood.

A rain of blood has blinded my eyes. Where is England?
  Where is Kent? Where is Canterbury?

O far far far far in the past; and I wander in a land of
  barren boughs: if I break them, they bleed; I
  wander in a land of dry stones: if I touch them
  they bleed.

How how can I ever return, to the soft quiet seasons?

Night stay with us, stop sun, hold season, let the day
  not come, let the spring not come.

Can I look again at the day and its common things, and

see them all smeared with blood, through a curtain
  of falling blood?
We did not wish anything to happen.
We understood the private catastrophe,
The personal loss, the general misery,
Living and partly living;
The terror by night that ends in daily action,
The terror by day that ends in sleep;
But the talk in the market-place, the hand on the broom,
The night-time heaping of the ashes,
The fuel laid on the fire at daybreak,
These acts marked a limit to our suffering.
Every horror had its definition,
Every sorrow had a kind of end:
In life there is not time to grieve long.
But this, this is out of life, this is out of time,
An instant eternity of evil and wrong.
We are soiled by a filth that we cannot clean, united to
  supernatural vermin.
It is not we alone, it is not the house, it is not the city
  that is defiled,
But the world that is wholly foul.
Clear the air! clean the sky! wash the wind! take the
  stone from the stone, take the skin from the arm,
  take the muscle from the bone, and wash them.
  Wash the stone, wash the bone, wash the brain,
  wash the soul, wash them wash them!

Good King, Bad Carol

Oxford Book of Carols

The carol that made King Wenceslas a 'household name' remains as
popular as ever in spite of this harsh verdict of the editors of the
Oxford Book of Carols, *Percy Dearmer, Ralph Vaughan Williams and*
Martin Shaw.

This rather confused narrative owed its popularity to the delightful tune, which is that of a Spring carol, 'Tempus adest floridium'. Unfortunately J.M. Neale in 1853 substituted for the Spring carol this 'Good King Wenceslas', one of his less happy pieces, which E. Duncan goes so far as to call 'doggerel', and the Rev. A.H. Bullen condemns as 'poor and commonplace to the last degree'. The time has not yet come for a comprehensive book to discard it; but we reprint the tune in its proper setting ('Spring has now unwrapped the flowers'), not without hope that, with the present wealth of carols for Christmas, 'Good King Wenceslas' may gradually pass into disuse, and the tune be restored to spring-time.

Good King Wenceslas looked out
   On the Feast of Stephen,
When the snow lay round about,
   Deep and crisp and even:
Brightly shone the moon that night,
   Though the frost was cruel,
When a poor man came in sight,
   Gathering winter fuel.

'Hither page, and stand by me,
   If thou know'st it telling,
Yonder peasant, who is he?
   Where and what his dwelling?'
'Sire, he lives a good league hence,
   Underneath the mountain,
Right against the forest fence,
   By Saint Agnes' fountain.'

'Bring me flesh, and bring me wine,
   Bring me pine-logs hither:
Thou and I will see him dine,
   When we bear them thither.'
Page and monarch forth they went
   Forth they went together;
Through the rude wind's wild lament,
   And the bitter weather.

'Sire, the night is darker now,
And the wind blows stronger;
Fails my heart, I know not how;
    I can go no longer.'
'Mark my footsteps, good my page;
    Tread thou in them boldly:
Thou shalt find the winter's rage
    Freeze thy blood less coldly.'

In his master's steps he trod,
    Where the snow lay dinted;
Heat was in the very sod
    Which the Saint had printed.
Therefore, Christian men, be sure,
    Wealth or rank possessing,
Ye who now will bless the poor,
    Shall yourselves find blessing.

The Great Royal 'Whodunnit'

Blind Harry, Nick Aitchison, Jim McBeth and Johnny McEvoy

In 1296 King Edward I deposed the Scottish King John Balliol and took away the Stone of Destiny, on which Scotland's kings had been enthroned since time immemorial. The Stone, reputed to have been brought to Scotland from Spain by way of Ireland by Galethius and his wife Scota, daughter of Pharaoh, was set beneath the Coronation Chair in Westminster Abbey, London, and there it remained for six and a half centuries until Christmas Day in 1950, when it vanished, creating one of the greatest royal Christmas mysteries of all time.

THE FIRST THEFT

The taking of the Stone of Destiny by Edward I was told by the fifteenth-century Scottish poet Blind Harry in The Wallace, *written in about 1477. This extract comes from William Hamilton of Gilbertfield's 1722 'translation'.*

King Edward and Corsepatrick march for Scoon,
And Scotland now sings a most mournful tune.
Few Scots were left, the kingdom to defend;
Then for the Baliol to Montrose they send;
And to their great and everlasting shame,
Do strip him of his royal diadem.
When thus depos'd, Edward usurps the crown,
And then, alas, all things went upside down;
Was crown'd upon the very self same stone
Galethius sent from Spain, with his own son,
When Iber Scot first into Scotland came:
Kenneth our king, and second of that name,
Brought it to Scoon, where kings in pomp and glore,
Were crowned for eight hundred years and more;
Even in that ancient royal marble chair,
So famous and so long preserved there,

Edward crossed the border and carried off the Sacred Scone of Scotland on which the Scottish Kings had been crowned for centuries, burying it with great solemnity in Westminster Abbey. From *1066 And All That* by W.C. Sellar and R.J. Yeatman; drawing by John Reynolds.

Which as a trophy, thence they do transport
To London, where King Edward kept his court.
But yet I'm told that ancient fates decree,
Where this stone stands Scots shall the masters be.

THE SECOND THEFT

On Christmas morning in 1950 Britain woke up to the news that Scotland's Stone of Destiny had been stolen – again! It had been taken from under the noses of Westminster Abbey staff and police by a group of students from Glasgow University led by law student Ian R. Hamilton. The incident is detailed in Nick Aitchison's book Scotland's Stone of Destiny.

On Saturday 23 December, Hamilton hid himself in the abbey after closing time, intending to wait until the early hours before forcing a door near Poets' Corner to admit the others and remove the Stone. But Hamilton was discovered by a night-watchman. Unaware of the jemmy hidden under Hamilton's coat, the watchman assumed that Hamilton was homeless and offered him some money before ejecting him from the abbey. But this setback did not deter the group. The following night, Christmas Eve, another attempt was made. At 4 am on Christmas morning they reversed one of the [two] cars [they had driven to London] up a lane beside the abbey and into a builder's yard beside Henry VII's Chapel. While [Kay] Matheson stayed in the car, the three men forced their way into the abbey through a door at Poets' Corner. From there they made for St Edward's Chapel, where they prized away the wooden bevel securing the Stone in its recess beneath the seat of the Coronation Chair.

So far, so good. But the group was then plagued with a catalogue of errors, though balanced by good fortune in equal measure. On pulling the Stone out of the Chair, it crashed onto the stone floor and, by Hamilton's own admission, broke into two pieces. The natural flaw in the rock, detectable on earlier photographs, had given way, detaching a corner – about a quarter of its total mass – from the Stone. The fragments were placed on an outstretched coat and dragged across the floor, down the Sanctuary steps, along the east aisle of the South Transept, and out through the Poets' Corner door; the Abbey authorities were able to trace the route the next morning from the tracks left on the floor. But the weight was considerable and, taking advantage of the mishap, Hamilton picked up the smaller piece and rushed it out to the waiting car where he placed it in the boot.

At that moment a policeman appeared out of the darkness. Hamilton and Matheson quickly feigned an embrace and, when questioned about their presence, claimed that they had arrived in London too late to find accommodation. The constable, taking pity on them, offered them cigarettes and, although a noise echoed from the abbey as [Alan] Stuart and [Gavin] Vernon wrestled with the rest of the Stone, he failed to investigate. After a smoke and a chat, the policeman advised them to move on. The two drove off with the smaller fragment of the Stone, leaving their compatriots with the remainder.

Hamilton soon returned to the abbey, leaving Matheson with the car and the lesser part of the Stone. But there was no sign of Stuart, Vernon or the bulk of the Stone. Emerging from the abbey, Hamilton stumbled across the broken Stone in the builder's yard outside. He then raced off to get the second car, which had been left in Millbank. Only when he got there did he realise that the keys were still in a pocket of the coat on which the Stone had been dragged from the abbey. Hamilton was forced to enter the abbey for the third time that night, this time searching on his hands and knees in the gloom for the keys, but to no avail.

Now desperate, Hamilton began to strike matches more in hope than expectation as the area to be covered was extensive. He had all but given up when he stepped on the keys. Retrieving the second car, Hamilton retraced his way up the lane alongside the abbey for the fourth time that night. Fuelled with adrenalin, he managed to lift the Stone into the boot by himself and drove off. Luck was still with them. In the Old Kent Road, Hamilton chanced upon a dejected Stuart and Vernon, who had abandoned their mission when they were unable to find the car keys. To avoid overloading the car, Vernon was left to make his own way home to Scotland.

Police issued a nationwide alert: 'Thieves with stolen Coronation Stone thought heading North by road'. Across northern England, off-duty policemen were hurriedly called from their Christmas lunches to man road blocks. All northbound traffic was stopped and searched in a huge operation to intercept the Stone before it reached Scotland. The Anglo-Scottish border was closed for the first time in centuries. But Hamilton and Stuart sped not north, but south. Successfully anticipating the police response, the pair drove around southern England, from Marlborough (Wiltshire) in the west to Rochester (Kent) in the east. Expecting to be arrested within hours they dumped the Stone in an open field on Christmas morning. But as the day wore on their confidence increased and they returned to retrieve their prize. The Stone was then hidden in a wood near Rochester before the patriots headed north. Not until Doncaster, 150 miles (240 km) north of London, were they stopped by police. But the pair talked themselves through and returned to a Scotland buzzing with news about the Stone's 'theft'.

The following week, Hamilton drove south again, on this occasion with another two companions, Bill Craig and Johnny Josselyn, and in a more powerful Armstrong Siddeley. But on returning to where they had concealed the Stone, they found a gypsy camp. After winning the gypsies' confidence, they retrieved the Stone. Substituting the Stone for the car's passenger seat, they concealed it beneath a travelling rug and, taking turns to sit on it, drove north. Travelling the back roads, they crossed the River Esk into Scotland between Longtown and Canonbie in the early hours of 31 December. The Stone was back in Scotland for the first time in 655 years.

THE SECRET REVEALED

The Stone was returned in 1951 as mysteriously as it had vanished – placed at the high altar of Arbroath Abbey, where Scotland's Declaration of Independence had been signed in 1320. It was taken south again, but was returned to Scotland with great ceremony on St Andrew's Day in 1996. And to the many legends that surround this symbol of Scottish kingship is now added another – was the one that was returned the true stone, or simply a copy? The background story was finally revealed in an article entitled 'Secrets of the Stone Uncovered' by Jim McBeth, which was published in the Scotsman *newspaper in 1996.*

Today, the papers compiled by Det. Insp. William Kerr of Glasgow Special Branch are in a black briefcase in a box on the shelves of Glasgow University's archives. The late Mr Kerr, who became Chief Constable of Dunbartonshire, gave them to Sir William Kerr Fraser, the former principal, more than 20 years ago. When Sir William retired last year he passed them to the university's archivist.

The story – hidden in witness statements, memos and investigation notes – begins with the removal of the stone, an act which, while it may have amused Scots, was no laughing matter at Buckingham Palace and the Home Office. Det. Insp. Kerr, in charge of the Scottish end of the police investigation, was put under 'almost intolerable pressure'. Every force in Britain was alerted but the focus was on Scotland, because a London bobby had spoken to a young man and woman with Scots accents near the abbey . . .

The first breakthrough came when a worker at a monumental sculptor's yard owned by the Glasgow councillor Robert Gray – who is no relation to the present-day councillor of the same name – reported he had seen the 'stone' in his boss's yard.

Mr Kerr interviewed Mr Gray, who has since died. He has been credited with repairing the real stone and making two copies.

Mr Kerr took the fake, but as he left he had an idea. He asked Mr Gray how he had known what the real stone looked like. The councillor said he had looked at a book in the Mitchell Library. The policeman thought the culprits might have done the same thing. His next step was to ask how many books about the stone were in the Mitchell and how many people had looked at them recently. He discovered there were three books and that two people had shown interest. The first was an African student who was discounted. The second was Ian Hamilton, a Glasgow University student and active nationalist, who had examined all three books on 29 November, 1949. Mr Kerr believed he had found his ringleader.

Next, the detective needed to track down the woman noticed outside the abbey. She had to be a friend of Mr Hamilton and a nationalist. He ordered a 24-hour surveillance on Mr Hamilton. A domestic science teacher, Kay Matheson, emerged as the front runner. However, discreet inquiries at Mr Hamilton's home in Pitlochry and Ms Matheson's Inverness-shire address revealed that both had apparently been at home during the Christmas holiday.

Mr Kerr persevered. He made inquiries at Ms Matheson's Glasgow school and learned that two days before the incident, she had made a large quantity of sandwiches. Mr Kerr believed they were made for the journey to London.

The next breakthrough came as Mr Kerr pored over piles of statements, one of them from an abbey watchman who had spoken to two Scots on the day before the theft. The pair had told him they came from 'somewhere with a name like Forgan'. The police settled on Forgandenny and Mr Kerr ordered a home address check on the university's 7,000 students. The names Gavin Vernon and David Rollo landed on his desk. Mr Rollo was not one of the conspirators.

Mr Kerr had the students watched and followed by police teams and student spies before deciding to confront Ms Matheson. He went to her home and accused her of being one of the thieves, which she denied. However, she was panicked into calling John MacCormick, a leading light among the Scottish nationalists. The result was that Mr Hamilton, Mr Vernon and another conspirator, Alan Stuart, arrived for a conference, watched by surveillance teams.

Mr Kerr turned his attention to the car. Mr Hamilton and Mr Vernon, he discovered, had hired a Ford Anglia. Checks established it had done 1,479 miles and a search uncovered one of two abbey door nails, which had been taken to be used as proof in negotiating with the authorities.

Mr Kerr took his evidence, photographs and documents to London where he met jubilant police and government officials. The four suspects were arrested and a report went to the Director of Public Prosecutions. Mr Kerr discovered Mr Hamilton had removed the stone, which was broken, by dragging it on his coat. The two pieces lay hidden, one buried near Rochester and the other in the home of a friend of Ms Matheson. Mr Gray is believed to have repaired the stone after the two parts were brought together in a house in Bearsden, near Glasgow.

Arbroath Abbey staff member James Wishart uncovers the Stone of Destiny after its return on 11 April 1951.

In a bizarre twist, the house was near Mr Kerr's home and its owner kept the stone for only one day because he misguidedly believed that a chance meeting with the policeman was proof that he was under suspicion.

On 11 April, 1951, after secret negotiations, the stone was handed over at Arbroath Abbey by three unknown persons. Two days later Mr Kerr personally took it to London, where it was accepted by the Dean, the Home Secretary and sundry VIPs.

A Mr Bishop, the clerk of works at the abbey who thoroughly examined the stone, concluded in a long report: 'My examination leaves no doubt in my mind that it is the Stone of Destiny, which was stolen from Westminster Abbey.'

Sir William Kerr Fraser said yesterday: 'I believe the real stone was returned. Councillor Gray attempted to persuade Mr Kerr that the returned stone was not genuine, but later agreed that it was. The replica differed from the stone in a number of ways.'

Sir William, who was a leading member of the students' representative council at the time of the removal, added: 'I remember great excitement. We were getting ready for the rectorial installation of John MacCormick and talk about the stone turning up at the ceremony was sweeping the place.

'I remember speaking to Hamilton and saying: "I hear you had a busy Christmas?" but he was playing it close to his chest.'

THE WEE MAGIC STANE

While the authorities in London and Edinburgh huffed and puffed much of Scotland laughed heartily at the 'prank' which had brought back Scotland's sacred Stone. This song, 'The Wee Magic Stane', written by Johnny McEvoy at the time, caused much mirth.

O the Dean o' Westminster wis a powerful man
He held a' the strings o' the State in his hand
And a' this great power it flustered him nane
Til some rogues ran away wi' his wee magic stane.
    Wi a tooreli ooreli ooreli ay etc.

Noo the stane had great powers that could dae such a
   thing
For withoot it it seemed we'd be wantin' a king.
So he called in the polis and gave this decree
Go and hunt oot the stane and return it tae me.

So the polis went beetling way up tae the north
They hunted the Clyde and they hunted the Forth
But the wild folk up yonder just pitied them a'
For they didnae believe it wis magic at a'.

Noo the Provost o' Glesga Sir Victor* by name
He was very pit oot when he heard o' the stane,
So he offered the statues that stand in George Square
That the High Churches might mak a few mair.

When the Dean of Westminster with this was acquent
He sent for Sir Victor and made him a saint.
'But it's no use you sending your statues down heah'
Said the Dean, 'but you've given me a jolly good idea.'

So he quarried a stane o' the very same stuff
And he dressed it all up till it looked like enough,
Then he sent for the press and announced that the stane
Had been found and returned tae Westminster again.

* Sir Victor Warren, then Lord Provost of Glasgow.

When the thieves found out what Westminster had done
They ran aboot diggin' up stanes by the ton
And for each one they finished they entered the claim
That this wis the real and original Stane.

But the cream o' the joke still remains tae be tellt
Fur the bloke that wis turnin' them aff on the belt
At the peak o' production wis sae sorely pressed
That the real yin got bunged in alang wi' the rest.

So if ever ye come on a Stane wi' a ring
Just sit yersel' doon and proclaim yersel' King.
For there's nane wid be able tae challenge yer claim
That ye'd crowned yersel' King on the Destiny Stane.

Twelfth Night

Bridget Ann Henisch, Hugh Douglas and Edward Hall

Throughout the Middle Ages Twelfth Night was the climax of the royal celebration. Usually referred to as Twelfth Day, it was a whole day spent feasting, hunting and enjoying mummers' plays. In her book Cakes and Characters *Bridget Ann Henisch explains that kings not only held court and wore their crowns on that last day of the Christmas festivities, but, paradoxically, often set aside*

their royalty to make way for a 'king' and 'queen' chosen from among their courtiers, and a Lord of Misrule to preside over the revels.

Like a magnet, the season drew to itself all kinds of performance, and Twelfth Day became the glittering finale. From at least 1302, when 'three clerks of the town of Windsor' entertained Prince Edward with interludes on the even of Epiphany, the stream of special celebration can be traced, growing ever broader and deeper until abruptly dammed up by the Civil War.

The core of a characteristic entertainment was simplicity itself. A troupe of mummers and musicians, splendidly dressed, would make a ceremonial entrance, delight the company with dance, pay their respects in dumb-show to the most important people present, and vanish as mysteriously as they had appeared. Sometimes a Narrator would accompany them, to explain the finer points of rudimentary story-lines, but he was of little consequence, except perhaps to the writer of his speech. The plot was just a wisp, a thread on which to hang the compliments and the costumes. A graceful compliment will never pall though often used, but for costume surprise was a note to be struck, and a disarming dottiness informed the proceedings.

During the Christmas season of 1347, groups of performers amused Edward III and his court, each set wearing a distinctive mask or headpiece, which ranged from an angel's face and silver halo to a mountain topped with couchant rabbits and, masterstroke of madness, one consisting entirely of legs waving in the air.

In Scotland they called this time the Daft Days and while the festival followed much the same pattern as in England, it was presided over by a 'boy bishop' and later by the Abbot of Unreason, Hugh Douglas writes in his book The Hogmanay Companion. *In spite of the Reformers' zeal to suppress such frivolities Mary Queen of Scots celebrated Twelfth Day with gusto after her return from France where she had grown up – and always attempted to outdo her rival Queen Elizabeth.*

France set her stamp on the festival [in Scotland] to give us customs and foods which today remain an inseparable part of the New Year festivities. By then the Yule festival . . . became known in Scotland as the Daft Days, a direct translation of the French *Fête des Fous*. . . . Even the monarch was not immune: in 1540 King James V watched as Sir David Lyndsay's play, *Ane Pleasant Satyre of the Thrie Estaites*, mocked the corruption in his government and the Church.

The fun ended on Twelfth Night, known as Uphalieday in Scotland, a day which saw a very special festival at the royal court, with guisers, dancing, plays and a night of endless revelry and merriment – all the enjoyments of Yule brought together into one great night of daftness to round off the Daft Days.

To choose a 'king' and 'queen' to preside over the Uphalieday festivities a rich cake was baked – the

A Regency engraving showing dancing around the Twelfth Cake.

ancestor of Christmas Cake and our traditional Black Bun – with a bean and a pea concealed in it. The man who discovered the bean and the woman who found the pea were declared King and Queen of the Bean for the evening. Two years after Mary Queen of Scots returned to Scotland from France, she 'abdicated' at the Twelfth Night celebrations and two of her Maries, Mary Beaton and Mary Fleming, took over as Queen of the Bean. In 1563 Queen Mary herself helped to dress Mary Fleming in her own royal robes and jewels, and the fun became so fast and furious that the English ambassador in Edinburgh, Thomas Randolph, was stunned by the extravagance of the occasion.

'My pen staggereth,' he wrote to the Earl of Leicester. 'The Queen of the Bean was that day in a gown of cloth of silver, her head, her neck, her shoulders, the rest of her whole body, so beset with stones, that more in our whole jewel house were not to be found.'

Henry VIII knew no moderation – in marrying, ridding himself of clerics and courtiers or in his Twelfth Day junkets, disguisings and tricks. A near-contemporary account of the first Twelfth Night of his reign in 1510, written by Edward Hall, describes a start to the revels that was unusual to say the least. It may have amused the gentlemen at court, but the ladies, including the Queen, were shocked.

The King came to Westminster with the Queene, and all their train: and on a tyme beyng there, his grace, the erles of Essex, Wilshire, and other noble menne, to the number of twelve, came sodainly in a mornyng, into the Queenes Chambre, all appareled in shorte cotes, of Kentishe Kendal, with hodes on their heddes, and hosen of the same, every one of theim, his bowe and arrowes, and a sworde and a bucklar, like out lawes, or Robyn Hodes men, wherof the Quene, the Ladies, and al other there, were abashed, as well for the straunge sight, as also for their sodain commyng, and after certayn daunces, and pastime made, thei departed.

Diverting King James

Dorothy Dunnett

Dorothy Dunnett's House of Nicolò series of novels recreates trade, power politics and war in fifteenth-century Europe. In To Lie with Lions, *the sixth book in the series, Nicholas de Fleury, founder of the*

Bank of Nicolò, finds himself in Scotland, deeply involved in European scheming. To divert the Scottish King James III (ruled 1451 to 1488) from becoming embroiled in wars in England and France he stages a lavish mystery play in Edinburgh for Epiphany.

For all the people around Nicholas – those who feared him, or loved him, or were anxious for him – that autumn in Edinburgh was a strange one. In the Castle the King, having commissioned the [Mystery] Play, watched his own dearest plans take second place to a spectacle. Silent, obedient, barren, the Queen saw it as well. . . . The more money the King lavished on this, the less there would be for any nonsense such as leading armies to France.

When the actors were chosen and the rehearsals began, advertised by the clang of the bell, the Abbot [of Holyrood] lingered to watch the men hurrying to and fro, their rolls under their arms. The rolls so carefully copied in his own cloisters, each man's part on a strip. Sometimes de Fleury came himself, brandishing the traditional baton of the Protocolle, the man who carries the book of the play and directs it . . .

The musicians practised where they had begun, in the collegiate church of the Trinity, learning the music as it was written. The singers had been joined by a child of fragile beauty called John, the son of one of the actors who, like his father, appeared on the recommendation of the abbot of Holyrood. Roger ['Whistle Willie' the court musician], who suspected everyone's musical taste but his own, heard the child once, and that night changed three pieces to accommodate him. His sister, equally angelic, was too young to sing but was given a role as a cherub. As for Will Roger himself, his condition varied through all this time between a state of violent happiness and violent anxiety. He forgot to eat, until the nuns noticed and began sending down baskets . . .

Hitherto, when set in the highest gear with every wheel spinning, Nicholas had been taking his share in a war, or contributing to a scene of international negotiation, or at the very least deploying a whip and reins to preserve the multiple concerns of his Bank during some heinous crisis.

Now he was exerting the same extreme concentration of skills for the sake of one brief event: an ephemeral work which, once over, would leave nothing behind it except, of course, bills. It was his belief and intention that, subjected to such an overwhelming concentration of effort, something unique might be born. Something not only unique but superb. Something not only superb but close to a vision he had, but had never put into words: something soaringly wonderful. From this area of his thinking, all cynicism, for once, was debarred.

He knew by now his own gifts. As the weeks went by and the hour of completion approached, he saw every task duly executed; the ocean tamed; the advancing waves drilled into order. In the days before the performance the lists shrank, ticked off one by one, and the shouting began to die down, and the yard of the Abbey of Holyroodhouse, veiled by its awning emptied of arguing men in cloth tunics, became a silken pavilion, a mysterious cavern where the spoken word lingered like incense, and trumpet peals mixed with the tassels, and a voice sang, inward and solitary, from a tunnel of cloud.

It was too soon to slacken, and too soon to hope, and too soon to wonder. Nicholas worked, smiling, even-tempered, a never-failing source of solutions and calm. During that last week he did not go near his business, but slept in snatches on a truckle bed in the Abbey, and ate what people put in his hand.

The Secrets had come. Many of the experiments were his own, devices to play on the senses. The lighting was put into place, misty, magical in the grey air; and the smoke in its dusky colours; and the palette of incense and spices. Below the covering turf, John's gleaming wheels turned without sound. Screened off, alone, Nicholas watched the Angel of the Annunciation spread his swan-wings and float, his yellow head bent, while his son's childish voice swayed at his side, a silvery air-thread in water. Nicholas stood, considering sound and its trajectories, and Will Roger walked about with him, and the players.

The costumes arrived. The actors, word-perfect, were permitted to leave their chambers of study and be shown to their places. Nicholas had sat by their desks many times. Now he used all his knowledge of them to help carry them through this last stage. The prompts and signals began to receive their rehearsal: he had not allowed the intrusion of placards. He had not permitted

anything which would destroy the fragile illusion: the awe, the pity, the beauty, the triumph of the birth of a child . . .

The day of the performance arrived.

From end to end of the town, the crooked streets were all empty; their inhabitants tumbled down to the foot of the Canongate and flushed up the mountain behind, as if the ridge were indeed the chute that Nicholas once had called it. The buildings lining the ridge were hung with banners, to honour the guests of the King.

It had come to James some weeks before that, instead of grudging the cost, he should be exploiting what promised to be the finest single work of prestige he could show, outside Mons Martha the cannon. One did not invite crowned heads to such an event. Those who came, however, represented their lords, and themselves were powerful noblemen, who would take back to their shires, their duchies, their kingdoms the reports of what Scotland could do. And when a funeral loomed, God forfend, or a marital feast, or a coronation, James would be pleased to consider the loan of his musicians, costumes and experts to those princes who lacked them.

The procession down from the Castle was a triumphant one therefore, despite a shower of rain; and the comfort of the royal stand, when they reached it, drew exclamations from the eminent visitors. They gazed at the face of the Abbey before them, hung with arras and garlands. They studied the silks of the awnings, the veiled and silent box of the stage in the centre below them. They were offered mulled wine and talked, while the benches were filled, and lamps and braziers glimmered, warming the air. From the well of the Abbey arena there arose the buzz of a beehive: the expectant murmur of two thousand curious souls. Then a fanfare of trumpets rang out, and the curtains raced back from the four walls of the stage, light as smoke. Behind them was Paradise, furled in sweet-scented clouds, beyond which glinted the slow-moving wheel of God's angels and the celestial throne, bright as the sun, with, kneeling beside it, a mighty-winged Gabriel. Then, from a core of dizzying radiance, the voice of God rolled, sending his herald to earth.

It had begun.

Many who were not present would later describe all that happened thereafter, for the report of it, borne on the wind, carried far. A man digging peats was petrified where he stood by the sudden silence as the curtains were drawn, and then by the gasp, and then the snatches of a single voice speaking, so terrifying and rolling and deep that he crossed himself. The voice stopped. Then the breeze slammed forth the peal of an organ, followed by a susurration like a wheatfield under rain, that swelled and swelled until it burgeoned into the voice of a full choir in song . . .

A play could take all day or a few hours. Your Nativities, with six or seven scenes, were sometimes over by noon, but not this one. It was the music. Not just the 'Ave Maria' and the 'Angelus ad Virginem' for the Annunciation, and a bit of something for the Salutation of Elizabeth, but a lot of singing no one had ever heard of before. And then when it came to the Shepherds . . . ! Everyone afterwards said it must have been during the Play of the Shepherds that the dance music came in, and between it the gusts of laughter, which you wouldn't expect.

Later, it came out that the shepherds were speaking in Scots, and making jokes that you wouldn't believe. Not that all the rest was in Latin, they said. A right mix-up of tongues, as if the story of Mary and Joseph belonged to everyone, as you could say that it did. The fun of the shepherds, they said, was what broke your heart when it came to the Manger, and the holy music was mixed with the lullaby, *Lully lullay, hail my bairn, hail my King, hail my darling.* You could hear that as well, from the hills.

Noon came and went. It rained a little, and ceased, and rained again. The peat-cutter worked slowly, cutting in rhythm. Across the marshes and plains, others

listened. At the Abbey of Holyroodhouse, the scenes
unfolded one by one. The Star burned. Glittering Herod
sent out his messengers and ripped the leaves from the
books of his lawyers, the fires of hell licking his throne.
Kaspar, Melchior, Balthasar spread their jewelled robes
and knelt, and myrrh and frankincense scented the wind.
Over Paradise, palace and stable the cloud banks
lingered and passed, tinged with sound; flushed with
close-woven plainsong; opulent with polyphony; pierced
by trumpets and clarions, dulcions and clarsachs,
schawms and viols: *Ne timeas, Maria*, Gabriel sang.

Instead of seedlings and moisture the wind distributed
words, and sighs following words – *Ave Gloriosa!*
swirling about the small hills: Craiglockhart and
Blackford and Braids, music fell like ash on their slopes;
and the voices of children – *pleni sunt caeli gloria tua* –
were borne by the stout vanes of seabirds winging from
Cramond to Bass. Watching them, men saw that the
underclouds carried thumbprints of light, and sudden
colours, and once a spray of crackling sparks, as if
someone had grated down a half-pound of thunder and
lightning, and tossed it for joy . . .

Towards the end, there was nothing but music: noble, expansive. The light blazed, and the Star, and the poetry ceased, giving way to the voices, at first transparent and low. The music thickened, beginning its climb. The secret trumpets suddenly burst into sound from the roof-tops, and the four organs began their low thunder . . .

On the stage, in the stands, nothing moved except a veil touched by the wind, or the threads of a child's hair, or the sudden spark of a jewel. The sound reached its apogee, vibrating through earth, flesh and bone, physical and spiritual at once; plangent, tender, triumphant. *Emmanuel!*

The paean stopped. The silence clamoured and raged, beating about in distraction like a soul torn from its casing and lost. Then it deadened and the people stirred, and moved, and made their opinion known. . . . Nicholas watched, and then turned the same smile to Gelis, who did not smile back. Then the royal party arrived.

He was used to it. Even at this extraordinary moment, he found the right tone, the right expression, the right words to deal with the chaotic mixture of raw sensibilities and royal formality. It was the same, after that, with everyone else who surged round him, securing him as in a clamp to the place where it had happened, although it was over. He became aware in due course that, although he had not escaped, at least he was mobile: that a phalanx of companions composed of his actors, engineers and musicians was moving him steadily away from the scene, and uphill. Just short of his Canongate house they formed a barrier and drew him through it, and forbade others to follow until he was indoors, in the Casa Niccolo, in his own house.

Will Roger was there, and Tom Cochrane, and John and Moriz and half the polyglot crew who had helped him to do what he had done. Will Roger said, 'Come, my bastard Flemish apprentice. Come, you amazing man. Come and get drunk.'

From that time on (people said), the sun and the moon shone out of the backside of Nicol de Fleury, and he could do what he liked. The king loved him. The people loved him. Only the Lord Treasurer cursed him on the quiet.

Christmas Birthdays

D.B. Wyndham-Lewis and G.C. Hesseltine, David Hilliam and Hugh Douglas

Life and death does not respect Christmas even among royals: King Richard II, King John and Bonnie Prince Charlie were all born around this time, and Edward the Confessor, Charles II's widow Catherine of Braganza, Queen Mary II and James Stuart the Pretender died then. The only member of the present royal family born during the festive season and living today is Princess Alexandra. She was born, not in a palace or castle, but at the family home of her parents, the Duke and Duchess of Kent, at 3 Belgrave Square, London, on Christmas Day 1936.

Froissart left us this account of the birth of the future King Richard II,
son of the Black Prince and Joan of Kent, at Bordeaux on 6 January
1367. It is taken from A Christmas Book; An Anthology for Moderns
by D.B. Wyndham-Lewis and G.C. Hesseltine, published by The
Orion Publishing Group.

I was in the city of Bordeaux and sitting at the table when king Richard was born, the which was on a Tuesday about ten of the clock. The same time there came there as I was, sir Richard Pontchardon, marshal as then of Acquitaine, and he said to me: 'Froissart, write and put in memory that as now my lady princess is brought abed with a fair son this Twelfth Day, that is the day of the three kings, and he is son to a king and shall be a king.' This gentle knight said truth, for he was king of England twenty-two year; but when this knight said these words, he knew full little what should be his conclusion. And the same time that king Richard was born, his father the prince was in Galice, the which king Don Peter had given him, and he was there to conquer the realm.

A CHRISTMAS BASTARD

Charles II had many mistresses, but the most notorious by far was
Barbara Villiers, or Palmer, to give her her husband's name, an ambitious,
greedy woman, whose sexual desire knew no bounds. She held great
power over the King to the disgust of courtiers and people alike. Barbara
Villiers gave birth to Charles's son at Oxford at Christmas 1665.

This had been the year of the great plague, with piles of corpses lying in the streets of London. Cries of 'Bring out your dead' echoed throughout the capital. Although Charles stayed in Whitehall longer perhaps than was prudent, eventually he decided to move his court to cities at a safe distance. He spent the months from October 1665 to January 1666 in Oxford – always a loyal haven for royalists.

Charles's long-term mistress Barbara Villiers, whom he created Countess of Castlemaine and Duchess of Cleveland, was staying at Merton College at this time, and caused much scandal on December 28 by giving birth to yet another baby boy. It was the third son she had produced for Charles.

The *Dictionary of National Biography* calls Lady Castlemaine 'a ravenous woman'. Charles gave her the most beautiful royal building in England, Nonsuch Palace, near Ewell in Surrey. It is to her everlasting shame that she promptly pulled it down and sold all the materials. Nothing remains.

From *Monarchs, Murders and Mistresses* by
David Hilliam

A NEW PRETENDER

Charles Edward Stuart, heir to the Jacobite Pretender, was born in Rome on 31 December 1720, his mother's pregnancy and confinement having been followed by every friend and enemy of the exiled Stuart royal family in Britain and on mainland Europe. For Clementina, the inexperienced young mother-to-be, accouchement

brought a long and difficult ordeal to an end. In Scotland Charles
Edward's birth was always celebrated on 20 December because
Britain had not yet adopted the New Style Gregorian calendar and
consequently was eleven days behind the rest of Europe.

Good news swept the Jacobite world during the Spring of 1720 – Clementina was pregnant. . . . The Queen, little more than a child herself and sadly lacking in knowledge of gynaecological matters, had no idea what pregnancy involved, not even enough to be able to hazard a reasonable guess as to when her child was due. James, no expert himself, was bewildered. 'The Queen returns to you her kind compliments and continues very well,' he wrote to the Duke of Ormonde on 11 November. 'It is indeed a little singular to have mistaken so much as 3 or 4 months in her reckoning.'

James's half-brother, the Duke of Berwick, was more understanding. He reassured the king: 'I do not wonder at the Queen's being mistaken in her reckoning, it happens often at first being with child, but I hope she will repair the delay, by giving us a prince at the end of this month.'

Clementina did not 'repair the delay' until the last day of the year. Soon after five o'clock on the afternoon of that New Year's Eve momentous news burst from the drab little Muti Palace in Rome: it raced across the city to the Vatican, and soon was winging its way to every part of Europe – Clementina Sobieska, wife of James Stuart, King over the Water, had given the Jacobite Cause a son and heir. As the child was born a great storm raged across Germany, laying waste the homelands of the

Electors of Hanover, and that night a new and brilliant star shone in the skies over Europe making the birth of the prince messianic. To Jacobites everywhere the star and the storm were omens: the fortunes of Scotland's ancient royal house had turned and one day this child would wear the crowns which were rightly his.

The boy was healthy and strong and he was truly the child of the Stuart sovereign: there would be no refuting that, no scurrilous insinuations that the baby was a changeling, smuggled into the queen's bedchamber in a warming pan, as had been spread when James himself was born in 1688. James had taken every precaution. The moment Clementina's first hint of labour manifested itself he invited the nobility of Rome and dignitaries of the Roman Catholic Church to be present, and they crowded the queen's room and the ante-rooms of the Muti Palace off and on for the best part of a week while the queen was in labour. There had been much coming and going at the Muti during the five days of the queen's labour, with everyone sent away when it was clear that the birth was not imminent, only to be summoned back almost immediately because it appeared about to happen. The Pope himself became involved in all the furore, visiting at the palace to give Clementina his personal blessing and offering up special prayers. More practically, he sent a supply of linen for the new baby.

When the Prince was born at last, the witnesses who pressed around Clementina's bed included cardinals representing Scotland, England and Ireland as well as the Vatican, France and Spain, and a host of noblewomen, most of them accompanied by their husbands – Lady Nithsdale, Donna Teresa Albani, the Duchess of Bracciano, the Duchess Salviati, and the widowed Principessa di Piombino with her three daughters, who were also escorted by their husbands . . . James himself knelt at a prie-dieu close to his wife's bed as his heir was born. . . . The baby was handed over to nurses, the Pope sent a present of money and holy relics, and the whole of Rome fussed around the new prince. By the time a royal salute echoed across the Tiber from the Castel Sant' Angelo next morning, the exhausted Clementina realized that the child she had borne, *her son*, was not hers at all, but belonged to a great royal dynasty of Europe and to the Jacobite Cause.

The names he was given confirmed this – Charles for his great-grandfather, Edward for England's only royal saint, Louis for the King of France, Philip for the King of Spain, Casimir for the kings of Poland, and the saints' names, Sylvester, to mark his birth on St Sylvester's Day, and Maria. He was rarely called Charles Edward: within the family he was known as Charles, although his parents – with typical inability to agree – used different names; James often called him by the Italian diminutive, Carluccio, while Clementina used the Polish form, Carlusu. The French called him Edouard, and the name Prince Charlie, which was to come later, was not a pet name but a rendering of the Gaelic *Tearlach* into English.

He was immediately created Prince of Wales.

From *The Private Passions of Bonnie Prince Charlie* by Hugh Douglas

Henry VIII's First Banquet

Margaret George

When the future King Henry VIII was seven he spent Christmas at Sheen with his father Henry VII, his mother Elizabeth and brothers and sisters Arthur, Margaret and Mary. All the love of the King and Queen was lavished on Arthur, a sickly boy who was heir to the throne, to the neglect of their other children, especially Henry, who was destined to enter the Church.

In her novel, The Autobiography of Henry VIII, *Margaret George describes that Christmas when young Henry experienced his first royal feast and the bitter taste of being a royal second son. But history had other ideas: Arthur died and the crown passed to Prince Henry, whose character was formed by such incidents as the banquet at Sheen.*

The festivities were to begin that evening with a banquet in the Great Hall. Then Nurse Luke informed me that Mary and I were not to go. I could understand why Mary must remain in the nursery – she was but two! But I was seven and surely should be allowed to go. All year I had assumed that when this season's Christmas revels began I would be part of them. Had I not reached the age of reason with my birthday that past summer?

The disappointment was so crushing that I began to howl and throw my clothes upon the floor. It was the first time I had ever shown an open display of temper, and everyone stopped and stared at me. Well, good! Now they would see I was someone to take notice of!

Anne Luke came rushing over to me. 'Lord Henry! Stop this! This display' – she had to duck as I flung a shoe at no one in particular – 'is most unlike you!' She tried to restrain my arms, but I flailed out at her. 'It is unworthy of a Prince.'

That had the wanted effect. I stopped and stood, quite out of breath but still angry. 'I want to go to the banquet,' I said coldly. 'I am quite old enough and I think it unkind of the King to exclude me this year.'

'A Prince old enough to attend formal banquets does not throw his clothes on the floor and scream like a monkey.' Satisfied that I was under control, she lumbered up from her knees.

Now I knew what I had to do. 'Nurse Luke, please,' I said sweetly, 'I want so badly to go. I have waited for it all year. Last year he promised' – this was pure invention, but it might serve – 'and now he makes me wait in the nursery again.'

'Perhaps His Majesty has heard about what you and Margaret did this afternoon,' she said darkly. 'Running ahead of the party.'

'But Margaret is going to the banquet,' I pointed out, logically. She looked at me and smiled and I knew I should have my way.

'I will speak to the Lord Chamberlain and ask if His Majesty would reconsider.'

Happily I began picking up the strewn clothes, already planning what I should wear. So that was the way it was

done: first a show of temper, then smiles and favour. It was an easy lesson to learn, and I had never been slow at lessons.

At seven that evening, Arthur and Margaret and I were escorted into the Great hall for the banquet. In the passageway outside I saw a band of musicians practising. They hit many sour notes and looked apologetic as we passed by.

As part of our education, all Father's children were tutored in music. We were expected to be able to play one instrument. This was a source of much struggle to Arthur and Margaret. I, on the other hand, had taken as readily to the lute as to horses, and loved my hours of instruction. I wanted to learn the virginals, the flute, the organ – but my tutor told me I was to wait and learn one instrument at a time. So I waited, impatiently.

I had expected the King's musicians to be well trained, and now disappointment flooded me. They were little better than I.

As we came into the Hall there was a fair blaze of yellow light. I saw what appeared to be a thousand candles on the long tables that ran along the sides of the hall, with the royal dais and table in between. There were white cloths for the full length of the tables and golden plate and goblets, all winking in the unsteady candlelight.

As soon as we entered, a man appeared at our sides and bent over and spoke to Arthur. Arthur nodded and the man – all richly dressed in burgundy velvet – steered him toward the royal dais where he would take his place with the King and Queen.

Almost at the same time, another man appeared and addressed himself to Margaret and me. This one was somewhat younger and had a round face. 'Your Graces are to be seated near the King at the first table, so that you may see the jester and all the mimes clearly.' He turned and led us through the gathering number of people; it looked to me like a forest of velvet cloaks. He escorted us to our place, bowed, and left.

'Who is he?' I asked Margaret. She had been at court functions several times before, and I hoped that she would know.

'The Earl of Surrey, Thomas Howard. He *used* to be Duke of Norfolk.' When I looked blank, she said, 'You know! He is head of the Howard family. *They* supported Richard III. That's why he's an earl now, and not a duke. He has to show his loyalty by seating the King's children!' She laughed spitefully. 'If he seats us often enough, perhaps one day he'll be a duke again. That is what he hopes.'

'The Howard family –' I began a question, but she characteristically cut it off.

'A huge, powerful one. They are everywhere.'

Indeed they were. Later I was to remember that until that banquet I had never heard the name. The Howard family. As King, I married two of them, executed three, and married my son to one. But they were all unborn that night, and I but a seven-year-old second son awaiting the day I must take clerical vows. Had I known what was to be, perhaps I should have killed Thomas Howard that night and forestalled it all. Or he, me. But instead he turned his back on me and disappeared into the crowd to pursue his business, and I propped myself up on one leg the better to reach the table, and the thing went forward as water running downhill towards its destination.

A sudden fanfare of cornetts and sackbuts (slightly out of time) broke into the babble of the assembly. Instantly the people fell silent. The musicians then struck a slow processional march, and the King, the Queen, and the King's mother filed slowly in, followed by Archbishop Warham, Lord Chancellor; Bishop Fox, Lord Privy Seal; and Bishop Ruthal, Secretary. At the very rear of the procession was Thomas Wolsey, the priest who served as the King's almoner. He must have had little to do, as the King was stingy and gave no alms.

She was here! My heart soared, and I could not leave looking at her – the Queen my mother. From earliest childhood I had been taught to revere the Virgin Mother, Queen of Heaven. There were figures of her in the nursery and every night I directed my prayers to her. But there was one image I loved above all others: an ivory one in the chapel. She was slender and beautiful and infinitely merciful, and had a sad, faraway smile.

Whenever I saw my mother, she looked so like the ivory figure that my heavenly mother and earthly mother merged in my mind, and I worshipped her.

Now, as I stared at her slowly coming into the hall, it was as though I were glimpsing Mary herself. I strained forward and felt myself becoming dizzy with excitement.

She walked beside the King, but her eyes were straight ahead. She did not look at him or touch him or speak, but walked on, ethereal and remote. Her robe was of blue, and her gold hair was almost hidden beneath her jewelled cap. She reached the dais. Arthur was beside her, and she reached out and touched his face and smiled, and they exchanged words.

I could not remember her ever having touched me thus, and the number of times she had spoken privately to me were fewer than my years in age. She had borne me easily and just as easily forgotten me. But perhaps this time, when we were alone for the gift exchanges . . . perhaps she might speak to me as she had just spoken to Arthur.

The King was speaking. His voice was thin and flat. He welcomed the court to Sheen. He welcomed his beloved son and heir, Arthur – here he made Arthur stand so that all could see him – to the revels. He made no mention of Margaret and me.

Servers brought us watered wine, and the courses began: venison, crayfish, prawns, oysters, mutton, brawn, conger-eel, carp, lamprey, swan, crane, quail, dove, partridge, goose, duck, rabbit, fruit custard, lamb, manchet and so on, until I lost count. After the lampreys I could take no more and began declining the dishes.

'You are not supposed to take more than a bite of each dish,' lectured Margaret. 'It is not like eating in the nursery! You filled your belly with prawns, and now there's no room for anything else!'

'I did not know,' I mumbled. I was feeling drowsy from the wine (watered as it was), the late hour, and my full stomach. The flickering candles before me and all up and down the table were affecting me oddly. I had to struggle to stay awake and upright. I hardly saw the grand dessert brought in, a sugared replica of Sheen Manor, and I certainly did not want any of it. My only concern was to keep from slipping sideways, lying down under the table, and falling fast asleep.

Then the tables were cleared and jesters and mimes came in for what seemed an interminable time. I could not focus on them and just prayed for it to be over before I disgraced myself by collapsing and proving Father right – that I had been too young to attend the banquet.

At last it ended. The jesters exited, tumbling and throwing paper roses and paste beads out over the spectators. The King rose and prodded Arthur to do likewise. No one in the Hall was permitted to stir until the Royal Family had left the dais, and I wondered what Margaret and I were to do as I saw the King and Queen, and Arthur making their way out.

Suddenly the King turned and, with a solemn nod, indicated that Margaret and I were to join them, He had known all along, then, that we were present.

A Feast of Carols

Robert Herrick

The royal banquet and mummers of Twelfth Day continued to be the apogee of Christmas through Tudor and Stuart times, in fact right up to the Civil War. John Leland witnessed the Twelfth Day feast in 1488 when 'at the Table in the Medell of the Hall sat the Deane and those of the Kings Chappell, which incontynently after the Kings first Course sang a Carroll'. Towards the end of Elizabeth I's reign 'children of the Chappell came before the Queene at Dinner with a Caroll'.

Robert Herrick (1591–1674), who began his career as an apprentice goldsmith before he joined the Church, was a staunch supporter of the Stuarts, and wrote several carols to be sung before King Charles I at Whitehall on Twelfth Night. Herrick's Carol from his Hesperides *was performed in the royal presence at Whitehall in 1647. This version is taken from the* Oxford Book of Carols.

What sweeter music can we bring
Than a carol, for to sing
The birth of this our heavenly King?
Awake the voice! Awake the string:

We see him come, and know him ours,
Who with his sunshine and his showers
Turns all the patient ground to flowers.

2 Dark and dull night, fly hence away,
And give the honour to this day,
That sees December turned to May,
If we may ask the reason, say:

3 The darling of the world is come,
And fit it is we find a room
To welcome him. The nobler part
Of all the house here is the heart:

4 Which we will give him, and bequeath
This holly and this ivy wreath,
To do him honour who's our King,
And Lord of all this revelling:

The First Night of 'Twelfth Night'

Leslie Hotson

Was William Shakespeare's Twelfth Night *first performed on Twelfth Night, and was Queen Elizabeth in the first-night audience? In his book* The First Night of Twelfth Night, *Shakespearean scholar Leslie Hotson makes a convincing case for this, although a last key piece of evidence is still missing.*

At Whitehall on 6 January 1601 Gloriana was entertaining a Russian envoy and a high-born Italian guest, Don Virginio Orsino, Duke of Bracciano, a member of one of Italy's most noble houses – a family almost as powerful as the Medici. Don Virginio was principal guest for the very good reason that in spite of the victories over the Armada both Italy and England still felt Spain to be a threat, and Shakespeare was doing his Queen a service (and himself no harm) by flattering her guest of honour – to the point of naming a character in his play Orsino.

On that Twelfth Night all three, the Bard, Gloriana and Don Virginio, were indulging in a scintillating piece of diplomacy, proving once again that monarchs had to attend to diplomatic business even during Christmas revels. Orsino went home at 2 in the morning, so stunned by all he had seen that he sat down and wrote a letter to his wife describing every detail – everything except the name of the play and the character who bore his own name. That was too delicious a morsel to pass on in a letter: he would wait, he told her, until he saw her to tell her about it.

Hotson printed Don Virginio's letter home.

Signora Consorte Amatissima,

On the Tuesday morning [6 January 1601] she [Queen Elizabeth] sent her coaches and two great ones [Lord Darcy, Mr William Cecil] to take me and carry me to court. Arrived there, I found at the gate the Earl of

Rutland, one of the first nobles of the realm, who assisted me to alight. He received me in her Majesty's name, and led me to a lodging appointed for me. I stayed there very little, and then went abovestairs, where I found a hall, all filled with waiting gentlewomen; another within, full of ladies and gentlemen, in the third were all the officers of the Crown, and Knights of the Garter, all dressed in white – as was the whole Court that day – but with so much gold and jewels, that it was a marvellous thing . . . The Queen came to the door, and I presently approached in all humility to do her reverence; and she drew near me with most gracious cheer, speaking Italian so well, uttering withal such fine conceits, that I maintain that I might have been taking lessons from Boccaccio or the Academy. Her Majesty was dressed all in white, with so many pearls, broideries, and diamonds, that I am amazed how she could carry them. The order is such that I am having the whole noted in writing; nor do I believe I shall ever see a court which, for order, surpasses this one . . .

After divine service, which the good Catholic Orsino declined to attend, came the banquet.

I was conducted into the hall where her Majesty was to dine: the which hall . . . was hanged with tapestries of gold. On a dais at the head was her Majesty's table; at the opposite a great court-cupboard all of vessels of gold; on the right hand a great cupboard of vessels with gold and jewels; and on the left, a low table with three little services for the Muscovite ambassador [Boris Godunov's envoy], and two who were with him; it being the custom of Muscovy that if he had not been seen eating in the Queen's presence, his great Duke would have had him beheaded . . .

After the feast Orsino returned to his lodging to rest, but returned to Whitehall in the evening.

The Queen came in, and commanded me to go along, discoursing with her. Her Majesty mounted the stairs, amid such sounding of trumpets that methought I was on the field of war, and entered a public hall, where all round about were rising steps with ladies, and diverse consorts of music. As soon as her Majesty was set at her place,

Queen Elizabeth dances with her courtiers. This anonymous painting is reproduced by kind permission of Viscount de l'Isle from his private collection.

many ladies and knights began a Grand Ball. When this came to an end, there was acted a mingled comedy, with pieces of music and dances, and this too I am keeping to tell by word of mouth. The Muscovite Ambassador was not present. I stood ever near her Majesty, who bade me be covered, and withal caused a stool to be fetched for me; and although she willed me a thousand times to sit, I would however never obey her. She conversed continually with me; and when the comedy was finished, I waited upon her to her lodgings, where there was made ready for her Majesty and for the ladies a most fair collation, all of confections. . . . After the Queen had gone into her chamber, those ladies who could speak Italian and French fell into conversation with me, and at the end of half an hour we took our leave of one another, and I went away home, it being already two hours after midnight.

Hotson was left as frustrated as we are. Orsino of Shakespeare's play remains as noble as the Queen's envoy, but was he intended to be Don Virginio? Hotson continues.

On seeing Don Virginio to bed – to the passing bellman's cry, 'Past two o'clock and almost three, My masters all, good day to thee!' – one's first unregenerate impulse is to wring his neck for not planning to put more about the comedy into his letter. But second thought reminds us that he acted precisely as we should have done in his place . . . saved the best and most fascinating detail . . . to tell his wife by gesture and by word of mouth.

A scene from a nineteenth-century illustrated edition of Shakespeare's *Twelfth Night* depicting Malvolio, Sir Toby, Sir Andrew, a clown and Maria.

Sentimentally, of course, we wanted the delighted Elizabeth to call up the modest poet-player for commendation. . . . But alas for our dreams – not a word, not a hint. . . . We may be confident, however, that a man of Don Virginio's curiosity and cultivation, with such a Queen . . . did not miss much that was written to his address in the play.

He [Shakespeare] had presented him as 'A noble duke, in nature as in name', desperately and poetically in love with the queenly-fair 'Olivia', and had her compliment him . . . with a plainly recognisable description, both handsome and not undeserved:

> . . . I suppose him virtuous, know him noble,
> Of great estate, of fresh and stainless youth;
> In voices well divulg'd, free, learn'd, and valiant,
> And in dimension and the shape of nature
> A gracious person.

Christmas is Cancelled

John Evelyn

Many thought the lavish overindulgence of King Charles I and Henrietta Maria at Christmas went far beyond the limits of morality and decency, but the King had even greater troubles. By the turn of the year 1641–2 he and Parliament were at such loggerheads that the enraged Charles marched into the House of Commons during the Christmas season determined to arrest five of the Members. This was a step towards Civil War for England and the scaffold for King Charles.

In Scotland in 1638 the Kirk's General Assembly forbade celebration of Christmas, and nine years later the Long Parliament in London followed its lead, abolishing not only Christmas but all other religious holidays. On the second day of January 1649 a court was set up to try King Charles. He was sentenced to death. This was a moment of truth for the monarchy and the age-old festival, as John Evelyn discovered in 1653 when he tried to mark the day of Christ's birth.

25 Dec. I went to London with my wife, to celebrate Christmas Day, Mr Gunning preaching in Exeter chapell, on 7 Micah v.2. Sermon ended, as he was giving us the Holy Sacrament, the chapell was surrounded with souldiers, and all the communicants and assembly surpriz'd and kept prisoners by them, some in the house, others carried away. It fell to my share to be confin'd to a room in the house, where yet I was permitted to dine with the master of it, the

Countesse of Dorset, Lady Hatton, and some others of quality who invited me. In the afternoone came Col. Whaley, Goffe, and others, from White-hall, to examine us one by one; some they committed to the Marshall, some to prison. When I came before them they took my name and abode, examin'd me why, contrarie to an ordinance made that none should any longer observe the superstitious time of the Nativity (so esteem'd by them)

I durst offend, and particularly be at Common Prayers, which they told me was but the masse in English, and particularly pray for Charles Steuart, for which we had no Scripture. I told them we did not pray for Cha. Steuart, but for all Christian Kings, Princes, and Governours. They replied, in so doing we praied for the K. of Spaine too, who was their enemie and a papist, with other frivolous and insnaring questions and much threatning: and finding no colour to detaine me, they dismiss'd me with much pitty of my ignorance. These were men of high flight and above ordinances, and spake spiteful things of our Lord's Nativity. As we went up to receive the Sacrament the miscreants held their muskets against us as if they would have shot us at the altar, but yet suffering us to finish the office of Communion, as perhaps not having instructions what to do in case they found us in that action. So I got home late the next day, blessed be God.

The King Can Dance Again

Samuel Pepys and John Evelyn

Christmas celebrations returned when Charles II came back to London with the Restoration of the Monarchy in 1660, but they lacked much of the splendour and gaiety of the old days – at least to begin with. The diaries of Samuel Pepys and John Evelyn provide a glimpse of this rebirth of Christmas after the Restoration. Pepys's diary for 25 December 1660 reveals little about Christmas.

To Church twice and dine on a good shoulder of mutton and chicken.

In his entry for 25 December 1661 Pepys makes no mention of Christmas Day, but he did go to church:

In the morning to church, where at the door of our pew I was fain to stay, because that the sexton had not opened the door. A good sermon of Mr. Mills. Dined at home all alone, and taking occasion from some fault in the meat to complain of my maid's sluttery, my wife and I fell out, and I up to my chamber in a discontent. After dinner, my wife comes up to me and all friends again; and she and I to walk upon the leads [paths].

While Pepys was preoccupied with his maid's sluttery and quarrelling with his wife, John Evelyn was watching the royal festivities.

Jan., 1st. [1662] I went to London, invited to the solemn foolerie of the Prince de la Grange at Lincoln's Inn, where came the King, Duke, &c. It began with a grand masque, and a formal pleading before the mock Princes, Grandees, Nobles, and Knights of the Sunn. He had his Lord Chancellor, gloriously clad and attended. It ended in a magnificent banquet.

Pepys's temper was little improved by Christmas Day 1662.

Had a pleasant walk to White Hall, where I intended to have received the communion with the family, but I come a little too late. So I walked up into the house and spent my time looking over pictures. . . . By and by down to the chapell again, where Bishop Morley preached upon the song of the Angels, 'Glory to God on high, on earth peace, and good will towards men.' Methought he made but a poor sermon, but long, and reprehending the common jollity of the Court for the true joy that shall and ought to be on these days, he particularized concerning their excess in playes and gaming, saying that he whose office it is to keep the gamesters in order and within bounds, serves but for a second rather in a duell, meaning the groome-porter. Upon which it was worth observing how far they are come from taking the reprehensions of a bishopp seriously, that they all laugh in the chapell when he reflected on their ill actions and courses. He did much press us to joy in these publique days of joy, and to hospitality. But one that stood by whispered in my eare that the Bishopp himself do not spend one groate to the poor himself. The sermon done, a good anthem followed with vialls, and the King came down to receive the Sacrament.

However, by New Year's Eve Pepys was in better humour.

Mr. Povy and I to White Hall; he carrying me thither on purpose to carry me into the ball this night before the King. He brought me first to the Duke's chamber, where I saw him and the Duchess at supper; and thence into the room where the ball was to be, crammed with fine ladies, the greatest of the Court. By and by comes the King and Queen, the Duke and Duchess, and all the great ones; and after seating themselves, the King takes out the

Duchess of York; and the Duke the Duchess of Buckingham; the Duke of Monmouth my Lady Castlemaine; and so other lords other ladies: and they danced the Branle. After that, the King led a lady a single Coranto; and then the rest of the lords, one after another, other ladies: very noble it was, and a great pleasure to see. Then to country dances, the King leading the first, which he called for; which was, says he, 'Cuckolds all awry', the old dance of England. Of the ladies that danced, the Duke of Monmouth's mistress, and my Lady Castlemaine, and a daughter of Sir Harry de Vic's, were the best. The manner was, when the King dances, all the ladies in the room, and the Queen herself, stand up; and indeed he dances rarely, and much better than the Duke of York. Having stayed here as long as I thought fit, to my infinite content, it being the greatest pleasure I could wish now to see at Court, I went home, leaving them dancing.

On 6 January Pepys went to the play.

To the Duke's house, and there saw 'Twelfth Night' acted well, though it be but a silly play, and not related at all to the name or day. Home, and found all well, only myself somewhat vexed at my wife's neglect in leaving of her scarf, waistcoat, and night-dressings in the coach today,

The Restoration of the Monarchy saw the relaxation of many of the rules and regulations that the population had been bound by under the Protectorate. People were able to pursue leisure activities such as those seen here – skating, bowling, shopping and games on the frozen River Thames.

that brought us from Westminster; though, I confess, she did give them to me to look after.

In 1663 Pepys does not mention Christmas at all on 25 December.

Lay long talking pleasantly with my wife, but among other things she began, I know not whether by design or chance, to enquire what she should do if I should by any accident die; to which I did give her some slight answer, but shall make good use of it to bring myself to some settlement for her sake, by making a will as soon as I can.

On the last day of the year, however, Pepys did have Christmas dinner, but it was a muted affair, with none of the dancing of the previous year.

We had dinner, my wife and I, a fine turkey and a mince pie, and dined in state, poor wretch, she and I, and have thus kept our Christmas together all alone almost, having not once been out.

In 1688 there was new turmoil. James II fled to France, leaving his kingdom to his daughter Mary and her husband William of Orange. These changes took place during the Christmas period, as observed by Evelyn:

18 [December] I saw the King take barge to Gravesend at 12 o'clock – a sad sight! The Prince of Orange: comes to St. James's, fills White-hall with Dutch Guards. . . . All the world go to see the Prince at St James's where is a greate Court, there I saw him and severall of my acquaintance that come over with him. He is very stately, serious, and reserv'd: The English soldiers sent out of towne to distance them; not well pleased . . .

24 [December] The King passes into France, whither the Queene and child wer gon a few days before.

Taking a Gamble

Bridget Ann Henisch, John Evelyn and the *Monthly Intelligencer*, January 1731

Gambling had always been a part of the royal entertainment since time immemorial, and as Bridget Ann Henisch shows in her book

Cakes and Characters, *it quickly became a feature of the revived Christmas.*

Just as the feast of Saturnalia was the one time in the Roman year when gambling was officially condoned, so Christmas in the medieval world was the recognized season for indulgence. In the fifteenth century a rule laid down for the Duke of Clarence's household decreed that no games of chance with dice or cards might be played for money except during the twelve days of Christmas. Even in the nineteenth century, when the most sedate families could play cards all the year round, a street-seller confided to Henry Mayhew at some time soon after the Great Exhibition of 1851: 'The sale of playing cards is only for a brief interval. It is most brisk for a couple of weeks before Christmas, and is hardly ever attempted in any season but the winter.'

Kings might choose to enjoy themselves at any time during the festival. Edward II once spent the holiday at Nottingham, and an urgent request for ready cash is recorded in his household accounts: 'To our Lord the King to play at dice on Chrismas night, by the hands of Sir John Cherleton, receiving money to carry to the King at Nottingham the same night, 5L [five pounds].' By tradition, though, as we have seen, of all the days in the season Twelfth-day was King's-day, and at court it was long the custom for the King to lead the gambling on that night. An announcement was made, 'His Majesty is out', and at this signal the King set aside ceremony and played as an equal with his companions. When he had won enough, or lost too much, he would give the signal for a second announcement, 'His Majesty is at home', on which he and his courtiers resumed their roles and it became less than diplomatic to go on winning against him. Play was deep, and both Pepys and Evelyn recorded in their diaries, with varying degrees of fascination and disapproval, the enormous sums won and lost at Charles II's court each January 6th.

The custom was well-established by the early sixteenth century and it was maintained until the year 1772, in the reign of George III.

At Twelfth Night 1662 Evelyn watched the King quite out of luck at the gaming tables.

This evening, according to costome, his Majesty open'd the revells of that night by throwing the dice himselfe in the privy chamber, where was a table set on purpose, and lost his £100. (The yeare before he won £1500.) The ladies also plaied very deepe. I came away when the Duke of Ormond had won about £1000, and left them still at passage, cards, &c.

Gambling was the rage, and King George II saw no incongruity in going from church straight to the gaming tables. After all, gold, which George adored, featured at both.

Wednesday, 6 Jan, 1731. This being the Twelfth Day his Majesty, the Prince of Wales, and the Kts Companions of the Garter, Thistle, and Bath, appear'd in the Collars of their respective Orders. Their Majesties, the Prince of Wales, and the 3 eldest Princesses, preceded by the Heralds etc., went to the Chapel-Royal, and heard divine Service. The D[uke] of *Manchester* carried the Sword of State. The King and Prince made the Offerings at the altar, of Gold, Frankincense and Myrrh, according to Custom. At night, their Majesties etc., play'd at *Hazard*, for the Benefit of the *Groomporter* [an officer of the Lord Steward's department of the Royal Household in charge of gambling], and 'twas said the King won 600 Guineas, and the Queen 360, Princess *Amelia* 20, Princess *Caroline* 10, the Earl of *Portmore* and the Duke of *Grafton*, several thousands.

The *Monthly Intelligencer*, January 1731

Georgie Porgie

Robert Cruikshank

Georgie Porgie pudding and pie,
Kissed the girls and made them cry.
When the boys came out to play,
Georgie Porgie ran away.

Who was Georgie Porgie of the nursery rhyme? There are many claimants – George I, Charles II and even George Villiers, Duke of

Buckingham. *The Prince Regent, son of King George II and later to reign as King George IV, was another none-too-popular royal suited to the title. Known as 'Prinny', he was amorous, amoral and a noted glutton. 'Prinny' usually ran away to Brighton, where he could have more fun in his very own brand-new palace. The Royal Pavilion began life as a farmhouse, but between 1787 and 1822 George turned it into a palace of fantastical Indian domes and minarets and filled with Chinese magnificence. Christmas 1818 promised to be miserable in London because of mourning for his mother, so 'Prinny' hied off to Brighton to entertain his friends at his almost completed palace. He was so carried away by his new state-of-the-art kitchens that he held a dinner below stairs shortly before Christmas, at which he carved the meat himself. George Cruikshank and other cartoonists had a field day, and the nation threw up its hands in horror when it read the report in the* Examiner *of 21 March 1819, quoting the* Brighton Herald.

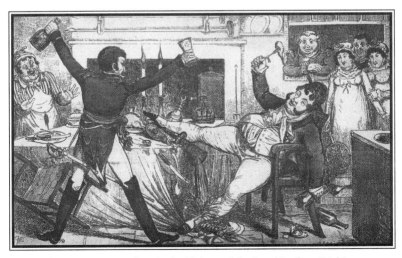

The Prince Regent's feast in the kitchens of the Royal Pavilion, Brighton, by George Cruikshank.

ROYAL FREAK – We are assured that, a few nights ago, the Prince Regent, in a merry mood, determined to sup in the kitchen of the Pavilion. A scarlet cloth was thrown over the pavement, a splendid repast was provided, and the good-humoured Prince sat down, with a select party of his friends, and spent a joyous hour. The whole of the servants, particularly the female part, were of course charmed with this mark of royal condescension. – 'Kings,' says Burke, 'are fond of low company.'

Right Royal Feasts

Elizabeth Craig, Royal Insight, the Royal Internet Website

'Georgie Porgie's orgy' in the Brighton Pavilion kitchens was the last of the great feasts which had developed during mediaeval times. By Queen Victoria's day Christmas dinner had become simpler fare, very similar to that of many ordinary families. Elizabeth Craig, who has studied royal tastes over the centuries, shows how the royal feast has changed over the years in her The English Royal Cookbook.

In mediaeval days, the Boar's Head crowned the feast. It was carried to the board on a silver dish, heralded with a flourish of trumpets, followed by a procession singing an ancient carol:

The Boar's Head in
   hand bring I
With garlands gay and
   rosemary,
I pray you all sing
   merrily.

James the First, who disliked Boar's head, is credited with substituting turkey for it at Christmas feasts.

The Royal Christmas fare of today has partly developed from the old-time fare. Yesterday crudely roasted thighs of deer kept Hotte Peacocke and Swan's Pie company at Royal Christmas dinners; in the days of Charles the First, five swans were sometimes roasted for the Royal Christmas dinner. Today roast goose or turkey reign king of the feast, and a sirloin of beef is often in attendance. Plum Pudding, which is not queen of the feast, is a royal descendant of Plum Broth, by way of Plum Pottage and Plum Porridge. It was not until the days of William and Mary that the original Plum Broth, which was served as soup in the days of Charles the First, and was composed of mutton stock, currants, prunes, raisins, sack and sherry, and later on was stiffened with brown bread, became known as a Plum Pudding.

In early days, no Christmas feast was complete without a most curious selection of pies, some filled with larks' tongues, some filled with seagull meat, some with lamprey and some with snails. These pies were originally made in an oval shape to represent the cradle in which the Holy Child was laid. During the feast, large flagons of spiced ale, called 'Lamb's Wool' were passed round. At the end of the feast, the Wassail Bowl was served, filled with hot, sweetened ale, cooked with roasted crabbapples and toast. The bowl was usually decorated with ribbons.

The Victorian Christmas dinner resembled a Tudor feast more closely than the Queen's festive meal today. In 1843 the Queen and Prince Consort spurned the more fashionable turkey for good old English beef.

Monday, Dec. 25, 1843.
At Her Majesty's dinner table, the chief dish, according to 'good old English custom,' was a splendid baron of beef, nearly four feet long, and between two and three feet in width, and weighing 180 pounds. There was also placed upon one of the side tables a hump of a Brahmin ox, presented to Her Majesty by Viscount Combermere, weighing 28 pounds.

From *A Diary of Royal Movements and of Personal Events and Incidents in the Life and Reign of HM Queen Victoria*, published 1883

By the middle of the nineteenth century, with a growing family and army of staff to feed, preparations for Christmas dinner at Windsor Castle had become a much more elaborate business.

The kitchens at Windsor Castle adorned with festive decorations, 1887.

An equerry visiting the Windsor kitchens (where 45 permanent kitchen staff worked) in 1860 watched the preparations for the Christmas feast. He noticed that at least 50 turkeys and a baron of beef weighing around 350 lb were being roasted at the fires. Hospitality was on a large scale, as shown by the traditional recipe for Windsor mincemeat, which included 82 lb of currants, 60 lb of orange and lemon peel, 2 lb of cinnamon and 24 bottles of brandy.

The kitchens prepared not only meals for the Royal Household, but also presents of food for workers on the royal estates and special friends. One such present was raised pies, which were labour intensive and involved four different kinds of deboned birds: a woodcock was put inside a pheasant, which was put inside a chicken, which was in turn inserted into a turkey – the whole was then surrounded with stuffing and rich pastry, so that each slice of pie had a cross-section of the different birds. The kitchen staff themselves enjoyed turkey, plum pudding, mince pies and roasted chestnuts.

From *Royal Insight*, the Royal Internet Website

At Osborne, Queen Victoria's favourite home, the Christmas menu had become much more elaborate by 1895, and a very rich and special plum pudding was served.

QUEEN VICTORIA'S CHRISTMAS DINNER

Osborne, December, 1895

Purée of Celery à la Crême
Cream of Rice à l'Indienne
Purée of Pheasant à la Chasseur

Soles Frites
Sauce aux Anchois
Woodcocks à la Robert
Quenelles of Fowls à l'Essence
Salamis of Widgeon à la Bigarade
Border of Rice garnished with Purée of Pheasant
Filet de Boeuf

Roast Turkey à la Périgord
Roast Goose à l'Anglaise
Faisans Gélinottes

Plum Pudding
Mince Pies à l'Anglaise
Pudding à la Gotha
Pudding de Cabinet
Nougats de Pommes
Tortes de Pommes à la Coburg
Gelée de Citron

On the sideboard
Boar's Head
Baron of Beef
Woodcock Pie

Wines
Sherry or Amontillado
Dry White Wines
Champagne and Moselle
Burgundy and Bordeaux
Malmsey-Madeira
Liqueurs
Port, Sherry, Madeira and Claret

(Balmoral Whisky and Apollinaris for the use
of Her Majesty who takes nothing else.)

From *An English Royal Cookbook* by Elizabeth Craig

The Christmas pudding is served, from *Little Folks, c.* 1870.

QUEEN VICTORIA'S PLUM PUDDING

This is the royal chef's recipe for the Christmas pudding served at
Windsor Castle during the early part of Victoria's reign. It comes
from Royal Insight, the Royal Internet Website.

Ingredients:- Three-quarters of a pound of raisins, three-
quarters of a pound of currants, half a pound of candied

orange, lemon and citron, one pound and a quarter of chopped beef suet, one pound of flour, three-quarters of a pound of moist sugar, four eggs, about three gills of milk, the grated rind of two lemons, half an ounce of nutmeg, cinnamon, and cloves (in powder), a glass of brandy, and a very little salt.

Method:- Mix the above ingredients thoroughly together in a large basin several hours before the pudding it to be boiled; pour them into a mould spread with butter, which should be tied up in a cloth. The pudding must then be boiled for four hours and a half when done, dish it up with a German custard sauce over it.

German Custard Sauce:- Put four yolks of eggs into a bain-marie or stewpan, together with two ounces of pounded sugar, a glass of sherry, some orange or lemon peel (rubbed on loaf sugar), and a very little salt. Whisk this sharply over a very slow fire, until it assumes the appearance of a light frothy custard.

The Making of Our Christmas

George Rowell, Elizabeth Longford and Godfrey and Margaret Scheele

Young Queen Victoria enjoyed going to the theatre, and the actor Charles Macready became a great favourite. However, when it came to pantomime-time during Christmas 1838–9 the lion-tamer was the star of the show.

The performer who captured the Queen's imagination at this time was neither actor nor singer, but a circus artiste. Her lifelong devotion to the circus dates from at least 1833, when a visit to Astley's Amphitheatre to see Ducrow, most dashing of riders, as St George in *St George and the Dragon*, sent her hurrying to her sketch-book to record her impressions. The Drury Lane pantomime for Christmas 1838 was *Harlequin and Jack Frost*, and included amongst its 'turns' Van Amburgh's Lions. The Queen may have set out for the performance on 10 January 1839 with no great expectations, for the pantomime 'was noisy and nonsensical as usual'. But in the eleventh scene noise and nonsense were forgotten: 'The Lions repaid all.' Although no Adonis ('he is a very strong man and has an awful squint of the eyes') Van Amburgh fascinated the Queen by his mastery of the menagerie, which included lions, lionesses, tigers, cheetahs, and leopards: 'They all seem actuated by the most awful fear of him . . . he takes them by their paws, throws them down, makes them roar, and lies upon them after enraging them. It's quite beautiful to see, and makes me wish I could do the same!' The notion of the Queen of England as a lady lion-tamer defies rational thought: nevertheless it suggests her growing appetite for authority.

Over a period of six weeks the Queen witnessed Van Amburgh's act seven times. On her third visit disaster threatened; part of the act was to place a lamb before the lion's nose:

which he as usual bore with indifference; when one of the Leopards, the smallest of all the animals and a sneaking little thing, came, seized the lamb and ran off with it; all the others, except the lion, and all those in the other cage making a rush to help in the slaughter. It was an awful moment and we thought all was over, when Van Amburgh rushed to the Leopard, tore the lamb unhurt from the Leopard, which he beat severely, – and took the lamb in his arms, – only looked at the others, and not one moved, though in the act of devouring the lamb. It was beautiful and wonderful.

On this occasion the Queen stayed behind after the performance to examine the beasts in their cages, which were brought back onstage for her inspection. She noticed Van Amburgh had 'a mild expression, a receding forehead and very peculiar eyes, which don't exactly squint but have a cast in them'. The Drury Lane management soon recognized their good fortune; when the pantomime ended, Van Amburgh and his Lions lent support to various operas, and the Queen sat impatiently through Rossini's *William Tell* and Balfe's *Maid of Artois* for 'what is to me worth more than all the rest'.

From *Queen Victoria Goes to the Theatre* by George Rowell

THE PRINCE'S CHRISTMAS TREE

Prince Albert quickly set his imprint on the royal festivities at Windsor, to the great delight of his young bride. And as their children were born he became determined they should enjoy Christmases like

those he and his brother Ernest had shared as boys. Consequently,
Windsor had all the trappings of a German Christmas.

December came with the present tables, and Christmas trees ordered by Prince Albert from Coburg. Queen Victoria was ecstatic about dearest Albert's innovation. Actually Queen Charlotte had set up a Christmas tree of Yew at Windsor before the beginning of the century, but the country acclaimed the idea as Prince Albert's and enthusiastically followed his lead. At Claremont he made Victoria a snowman twelve feet high, played Blind Man's Buff with the ladies and taught them a delightful new round game, *Nain Jaune*. There was also *Loto Dauphine*, *Maccoo*, *Speculation* and *Vingt-et-Un*, on which a gentleman once won a guinea. *Maccoo*, his brother Ernest's introduction, was too much of a wild gamble to please the Queen.

Prince Albert was the dextrous coachman of the family sledge jingling across the snow with grey ponies and scarlet grooms, the knight of Victoria's ice-chair, the champion skater on Frogmore pond. How she admired the elegant swan's head at the tip of each skate. When he slipped down playing ice-hockey she was amazed at the agility with which he sprang to his feet again . . . Christmas entertainments held for Queen Victoria all the happiness in the world.

From *Victoria R.I.* by Elizabeth Longford

Writing to his step-mother on 26 December 1847, Prince Albert remarked, 'I must now seek in the children an echo of what Ernest [his brother] and I were in the old

Christmas trees and tables laden with gifts ready for the royal family's celebrations in the Durbar Room, Osborne House, 1896.

time, of what we felt and thought; and their delight in the Christmas-trees is not less than ours used to be.'

From early childhood both Queen Victoria and Prince Albert rejoiced in a Christmas eve 'entirely German and *gemutlich*', when gifts, laid out on individual tables, were exchanged in the radiant glow of candle-lit trees. After the present-giving the candles were extinguished, to be relit on Christmas Day, on New Year's Day and on Twelfth Night when gingerbread was an established feature of the decoration. Trees hung with sweetmeats, fruits and toys and illuminated with small wax candles were known at the Christmas parties of Queen Charlotte, consort of George III, of Queen Adelaide and of the Duchess of Kent. It was left, however, to Prince Albert and Queen Victoria to establish the tree as a popular symbol, the Queen making a special point of presenting trees to barracks and schools where children's parties were being held.

From *The Prince Consort: Man of Many Facets* by
Godfrey and Margaret Scheele

Christmas Without Albert

Letters and Journals of Queen Victoria and Elizabeth Longford

Together, Queen Victoria and Prince Albert had created a family Christmas, which was a highlight of each of their twenty-one happy

years together. Albert's unexpected death on 14 December 1861 left
the Queen devastated – doubly so because it occurred very close to
Christmas. She was so consumed by grief she could not even attend
his funeral, and as for Christmas, on Christmas Eve she poured out
her sorrow to her beloved Uncle Leopold.

Osborne, 24th December 1861

My Beloved uncle, – Though, please God! I am to see
you so soon, I must write these few lines to prepare you
for the trying, sad existence you will find it with your
poor forlorn, desolate child – who drags on a weary,
pleasureless existence! I am also anxious to repeat *one*
thing, and that one is my firm resolve, my irrevocable
decision, viz. That his wishes – his plans about
everything, his views about everything are to be my law!
And no human power will made me swerve from what
he decided and wished, – and I look to you to support
and help me in this. I apply this particularly as regards
our children – Bertie, etc. – for whose future he had
traced everything so carefully. I am also determined that
no one person, may he be ever so good, ever so devoted
among my servants – is to lead or guide or dictate to me.
I know how he would disapprove it. And I live on with
him, for him; in fact I am outwardly separated from him,
and only for a time.

No one can tell you more of my feelings, and can put
you more in possession of many touching facts than our
excellent Dr Jenner, who has been and is my great
comfort, and whom I would entreat you to go see and

hear before you see any one else. Pray do this, for I fear much others trying to see you first and say things and wish for things which I should not consent to.

Though miserable weak and utterly shattered, my spirit rises when I think any wish or plan of his is to be touched or changed, or I am made to do anything. I know you will help me in my utter darkness. It is but a short time, and then I go – never, never to part! Oh! that blessed, blessed thought! He seems so near to me, so quite my own now, my precious darling! God bless and persevere you.

Ever your wretched but devoted Child,

Victoria

What a Xmas! I won't think of it.

From *The Letters of Queen Victoria*, edited by A.C. Benson

At last, on New Year's Day 1862, the Queen was able to put pen to paper in her Journal again.

Have been unable to write my Journal since the day my beloved one left us, and with what a heavy broken heart I enter on a new year [at Osborne] without him! My dreadful and overwhelming calamity gives me so much to do, that I must henceforth merely keep notes of my sad and solitary life. This day last year found us so perfectly happy, and now! Last year music woke us; little gifts, new years wishes, brought in by maid, and then given to dearest Albert, the children waiting with their gifts in the next room – all these recollections were pouring in on my mind in an overpowering manner. Alice slept in my room, and dear baby [Princess Beatrice, the queen's youngest child] came down early. Felt as if living in a dreadful dream. Dear Alice much affected when she got up and kissed me. Arthur gave me a nosegay, and the girls, drawings done by them of their dear father and me. Could hardly touch my breakfast.

When dressed saw Dr Jenner, Mr. Ruland [Librarian at Windsor], and Augusta Bruce [Resident Bedchamber Woman to the Queen]. Went down to see the sketch for a statue of my beloved Albert in Highland dress, which promises to be good. Then out with Lenchen [her former governess], Toward [Land Steward at Osborne] always following and pointing out trees and everything. When I came in, saw the Duke of Newcastle [Colonial Secretary] in dear Albert's room, where all remains the same. Talking for long of him, of his great goodness, and purity, quite unlike anyone else. Saw Sir J. Clark, Sir C. Phipps [Keeper of her Majesty's Privy Purse], and then dear, kind Uncle Leopold.

From *Queen Victoria in her Letters and Journals*,
edited by Christopher Hibbert

Christmas was a subdued affair during the remainder of Queen Victoria's life, with little of the fun of Albert's day. Bertie and his family cannot be blamed for preferring the enjoyments of Sandringham to the sadness of Osborne, which is apparent in this extract from the Queen's Journal for 1 January 1887.

1 January 1887 A small family party for New Year, quite unusually so. Only Beatrice and Liko [Prince Henry of

The residents of Sandringham would have enjoyed a Christmas house party like the one depicted in this drawing from 1895. By this time, however, Queen Victoria preferred the more solemn atmosphere she had created at Osborne House.

Battenberg, Beatrice's husband], but the children were there. Gave each other cards; even the sweet little baby, who was brought in, had one tied to a string round his little arm. Telegrams pouring in and being sent out, and letters and cards innumerable. Bertie most kindly sent me a Jubilee inkstand, which is the first that has yet been sold. It is the crown, which opens and on the inside there is a head of me.

From *Queen Victoria in her Letters and Journals*, edited by Christopher Hibbert

Although nursing her personal sorrows, Victoria continued to cling to power at home and abroad. She was well aware that she had to

accept government decisions as final, but fought to the bitter end to have her way. She was proclaimed Empress of India on 1 January 1877 – without even telling Bertie, her heir, who was at that moment in India on a tour to heal the wounds of the Mutiny.

At the end of 1895 after the disastrous Jameson Raid, which led to the Boer War, Victoria's grandson, the Kaiser, sent a telegram to President Kruger congratulating him on his success against the British. The old Queen was furious with 'Willie' and told him so.

5 January 1896

As your Grandmother to whom you have always shown so much affection and of whose example you have always spoken with so much respect, I feel I cannot refrain from expressing my deep regret at the telegram you sent President Kruger. It is considered very unfriendly towards this country, which I feel sure it is not intended to be, and has, I grieve to say, made a very painful impression here. The action of Dr. Jameson was of course very wrong and totally unwarranted; but considering the very peculiar position in which the Transvaal stands towards Great Britain, I think it would have been far better to have said nothing.

From *The Letters of Queen Victoria, Third Series 1886–1901*, edited by G.E. Buckle

In July 1900 the old Queen wrote, 'It is a horrible year, nothing but sadness & horrors of one kind & another.' She continued to carry out a few duties until Christmas when it was time to leave Windsor for Osborne.

The magic of Osborne now failed her. She fell into an erratic, unaccustomed routine which irritated her enormously. She would go to bed exhausted at 10 pm. Draughts of chloral and Benger's food would then prove insufficient to send her to sleep. After hours of tossing she would fall into a drugged slumber not awaking until noon. The whole morning would thus have been 'wasted'. Her afternoon drive would be spoilt by a fresh access of overwhelming sleepiness, her evenings by the inexorable task of signing papers and dictating her letters and Journal. For the past year or so her ladies had succeeded in keeping her awake in her carriage by constantly rearranging her mantles. Now her drowsiness was invincible. On Christmas Eve she went into the Durbar Room for the Christmas tree. There was no sparkle, the candles seemed dim. 'I felt very melancholy as I see so very badly.' On Christmas Day it was gradually broken to her that her last intimate friend of nearly fifty years, Lady Churchill, had died from heart failure in the night. 'Beloved Jane' was carried to the mainland on the night of the 28th in a fearful tempest. Queen Victoria lay shivering in agony lest the ship should founder.

The 'horrible year' blew itself out in a wail of wind and rain. For the first time the Queen allowed a new year to crawl in without a good resolution. 'Another year begun & I am feeling so weak and unwell that I enter upon it sadly.' But Lord Salisbury received his New Year card as usual, a pathetically appropriate one – *'The Old Year dies; God beckons those we love'* – signed with a quavering hieroglyph which stood for the once proud V.R.I. Nor would she admit to her stricken daughter, the Empress Frederick, that she had given up. In her last letter (6 January) she hoped soon to 'improve'.

From *Victoria R.I.* by Elizabeth Longford

There was to be no improvement. Queen Victoria died on the evening of 22 January 1901.

Indian Whoops from Canada

Punch, December 1843

At Christmas 1843 a group of Ojibbeway Indians from 'the wilds of America' on the northern shore of Lake Huron in Upper Canada proved a great attraction at the Egyptian Hall, Piccadilly. They were invited to Windsor Castle to perform before the Queen and Prince Albert. They danced naked to the waist but, as the Queen said, what with their war-paint, beads and dark skins, 'one does not really notice it'.

On their arriving at Windsor, the porter, in his red and gold livery, was hailed with a most unanimous whoop of delight from the whole party. They declared they had come expecting to see the great Mother, as they called the Queen, but that they had found the great grandfather Sykes, the porter, who was instantly converted into a sort of Maypole, round which the party went through one of

Indians performing the scalp dance, from the *Boy's Own Paper Annual*, 1885.

their national war dances – occasionally illustrating some Indian manoeuvres by pokes with their tomahawks, and evolutions with their scalping-knives. Sykes, who was glad enough to get rid of them, handed them over to one of the pages, who ran up the great staircase with the whole tribe at his heels, indulging in one of their national yells . . .

The moment the Ojibbeways got into the apartment where the Queen was expecting them, Ah-que-we-zaintz ('the Boy', as the interpreter called him, though he was above 70 years old . . .) made the following very strong observations, which we give in all their native strength and purity.

Wha cke ou ded ow fold erod ed id dle rowd ed ow tolderi ddeir id o.

It was explained to her Majesty that 'the boy' merely meant to say that he was too unwell to say anything. The War-chief then made a few remarks in Ojibbeway, which were translated into gibberish by Strong-wind – who called himself the interpreter. . . . The War-chief was understood to say that he was glad to see the faces of the English all wearing pleasant looks; upon which her Majesty observed, that 'the gentleman in beads and feathers could not have seen a Tax-collector, or he would not have described all the English faces as pleasant'. The War-chief alluded to the size of her Majesty's wig-wam – the name he was pleased to bestow on Windsor Castle. When the Queen good naturedly suggested that 'if it was any wam, it was a Tory and not a Whig wam, since the change in the ministry'.

The War-chief then gave a very broad hint which was not taken. He remarked that presents had often been sent them from this country – but her Majesty having no loose cash about her, did not act upon the suggestion of Pattona-quotta-weebe, for such was the name of the unfathomable and venerable rasper (deep old file) who had been addressing her. The Party then went through several of their dances, in which Weenish-ka-weebe – the 'Flying Gull' – greatly distinguished himself.

We are sorry that the Ojibbeways are so hard up as to be reduced to public exhibition at so much a head – for we should feel the degradation deeply, if any of our English warriors were abroad in the same predicament. Fancy the Duke of Wellington and the Marquis of Anglesey finding themselves short of cash somewhere at the other end of the world, and performing the broad-sword exercise before an audience of native Indians, for the purpose of paying their expenses home again. Or, suppose it possible that any of our Royal Family should get out to Ojibbeway, and go through the dances of their country – a Scotch reel, an Irish jig, or an English naval hornpipe, for the amusement of the court people. Such, however, appears to be the degrading position in this country, of the chiefs of the tribe of the Ojibbeway Indians.

From *Punch*, December 1843

An American Carol

John Henry Hopkins

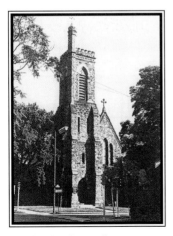

The church at Williamsport, Pennsylvania, USA, where Dr Hopkins was rector.

One of the world's favourite Christmas carols was composed by an American clergyman and noted hymn-writer, Dr J.H. Hopkins. He was rector of Christ's Church, Williamsport, Pennsylvania, at the time he composed 'We Three Kings of Orient Are' in the 1850s. He died at Troy, New York, in 1891. This version of the carol is taken from the Oxford Book of Carols.

'We Three Kings of Orient Are'

The Kings.
We three kings of Orient are;
Bearing gifts we traverse afar
Field and fountain, moor and mountain,
Following yonder star:

O star of wonder, star of night,
Star with royal beauty bright,
Westward leading, still
proceeding,
Guide us to thy perfect light.

Melchior.
Born a king on Bethlehem
plain,
Gold I bring to crown him
again–
King for ever, ceasing never,
Over us all to reign: *O star of*
wonder, star of night

Dr John Henry Hopkins.

Caspar.
Frankincense to offer have I;
Incense owns a Deity nigh:
Prayer and praising, all men raising,
Worship him, God most high: *O star of*
wonder, star of night

Balthazar.

Myrrh is mine; its bitter perfume

Breathes a life of gathering gloom;

Sorrowing, sighing, bleeding, dying,

Sealed in the stone-cold tomb: *O star of*
wonder, star of night

All.

Glorious now behold him arise,

King, and God, and sacrifice!

Heaven sings alleluya,

Alleluya the earth replies: *O star of*
wonder, star of night

Bicentennial Message to the USA

HM Queen Elizabeth II

One of the most memorable Christmas broadcasts made by
Queen Elizabeth II was that of 1976, following her visit to the USA
during the celebrations to mark the bicentenary of the signing of the
Declaration of Independence.

Christmas is a time for reconciliation. A time not only for families and friends to come together but also for differences to be forgotten.

In 1976 I was reminded of the good that can flow from a friendship that is mended. Two hundred years ago the representatives of the thirteen British colonies in North America signed the Declaration of Independence in Philadelphia.

This year we went to America to join in their Bicentennial Celebrations. Who would have thought two hundred years ago that a descendant of King George III could have taken part in these Celebrations? Yet that same King was among the first to recognise that old scores must be settled and differences reconciled and the first United States Ambassador to Britain declared that he wanted 'the old good nature and the old good humour restored'.

And restored they were. The United States was born in bitter conflict with Britain but we didn't remain enemies for long. From our reconciliation came incalculable benefits to mankind and a partnership which, together with many countries of the Commonwealth, was proved in two World Wars and ensured that the light of liberty was not extinguished.

King George III never saw the Colonies he lost. My father, King George VI, was the first British sovereign to see the famous skyline of Manhattan and to visit the rich and vibrant country that lies beyond it.

Wherever we went the welcome was the same, all the way to Boston where the first shots in the war between Britain and America were fired.

Reconciliation, like the one that followed the American War of Independence, is the product of reason, tolerance, and love and I think that Christmas is a good time to reflect on it.

It is easy enough to see where reconciliation is needed and where it would heal and purify, obviously in national and international affairs, but also in homes and families.

A few weeks ago, for instance, I met in my home a group of people who are working for better understanding between people of different colour, different faiths, and different philosophies – and who are trying to solve the very real problems of community relations.

It is not something that is easy to achieve. But things that are worthwhile seldom are, so it is encouraging to know that there are many people trying to achieve it.

Another shining example is the peace movement in Northern Ireland. Here Roman Catholics and Protestants have joined together in a crusade of reconciliation to bring peace to the Province.

Next year is a rather special one for me and I would like my Silver Jubilee year also to become a special one for people who find themselves the victims of human conflict. The gift I would most value next year is that reconciliation should be found wherever it is needed. A reconciliation which would bring peace and security to families and neighbours at present suffering and torn apart.

Remember that good spreads outwards and every little does help. Mighty things from small beginnings grow as indeed they grew from the small child of Bethlehem.

I believe there is another thought from which we can draw encouragement. If there is reconciliation – if we can get the climate right – the good effects will flow much more quickly than most people would believe possible. Those who know the desert know also how quickly it can flower when the rains come. But who in Britain who saw the parched earth and empty reservoirs last summer would have believed that the grass would grow so strong, so green, and so soon when the drought ended? When the conflict stops, peace can blossom just as quickly.

I wish you all a very happy Christmas and may the New Year bring reconciliation between all people.

Greetings to the World

Tom Fleming, HM George V, HM George VI and HM Elizabeth II

The sovereign's broadcast is as much a part of Christmas as plum pudding and crackers, and has been ever since King George V first spoke to the nation on Christmas Day 1932. Few years have been missed: in 1936, a fortnight after the abdication of Edward VIII (however, the new King, George VI, spoke a short message on New Year's Day); in 1938 the then Prime Minister Neville Chamberlain, for some incredible reason, thought a Christmas broadcast inappropriate; and in 1969, when the Queen's speech was replaced by a documentary about the life of the royals.

It took the then head of the BBC John Reith ten years to persuade Buckingham Palace to agree to make that first broadcast but without it, Christmas would not be Christmas for many people around the world.

GEORGE V – A VOICE OUT OF THE AIR

The King was, as usual, to be spending a family Christmas [in 1932] at his beloved Sandringham. ('I have a house in London, and a home at Sandringham,' he had been heard to say on more than one occasion.) The time chosen for the broadcast was 3 pm, because that was the most advantageous time for reaching most of the Empire countries by short waves from the transmitters in Britain. The room chosen as 'the broadcasting room' by BBC engineers was 'an ugly little room' on the ground floor, the office of the Master of the Household, in a corner underneath the staircase. The King agreed to do some voice tests to choose a position for the small table which would hold the microphones in front of his favourite wicker armchair. (Just before the actual broadcast, it seems, he sat down too heavily, went through the seat of the chair, and exclaimed – with regal restraint – 'God bless my soul!')

The control room was set up in an adjoining room, the office of the Clerk to the Keeper of the Privy Purse. The microphones and other equipment, sent from Broadcasting House on 22nd December, were installed at Sandringham by a small team of four engineers. Contrary to Press reports in the previous week, a 'special golden microphone' was not included in the technical requirements. There were three neat square cases of Australian walnut – two large, to house the microphones (previously hung in a London cinema, and carefully cleaned and fitted with new silk to cover the diaphragms

George V prepares to give the 1934 Christmas radio broadcast from Sandringham.

for their Royal début) and a smaller, to cover the red cue-light. . . . The microphones were completely hidden by the walnut cases, and there were small openings, three inches long and two inches wide, covered with gauze through which The King's voice reached them. The small table at which he sat had been furnished with a table-cloth at the BBC men's request. A note to the Private Secretary stressed that 'noises made by drawing the script across the table-cloth, or rustling, or crackling it while reading are greatly exaggerated when broadcast. We would be grateful if precautions were taken to avoid this . . .'. The King was given no other lessons in the art of broadcasting. He was reminded of the light signals (flashing red to stand-by; permanent red meaning 'on the air') by a little card specially printed and placed by the cue-light case. (He preferred to be cued by hand – often a tap on the shoulder.) He was very nervous about broadcasting, and had taken immense trouble with his choice of simple, easy language. He listened to many of the messages of greeting from around the Empire which preceded his broadcast on his own wireless set, and came to the 'broadcasting room' at a quarter to three. At five past three, the red light flashed and glowed, and The King, after a pause of six seconds, spoke his first words, artlessly and naturally, a broadcaster to the manner born. In his journal he noted 'I went to Francis's room, and at 3.35 pm broadcasted 251 words to the Empire'. (Francis was Lord Knollys, who had been The King's Joint Private Secretary at the beginning of his reign, and who had died eight years before, in 1924. The time quoted was 'Sandringham' time. The King, like his father, a stickler for punctuality, kept all the clocks half-an-hour ahead of Greenwich Mean Time!)

From *Voices out of the Air* by Tom Fleming

This is what the King said in that first broadcast in 1932.

Through one of the marvels of modern Science, I am enabled, this Christmas Day, to speak to all my peoples throughout the Empire. I take it as a good omen that Wireless should have reached its present perfection at a time when the Empire has been linked in closer union. For it offers us immense possibilities to make that union closer still.

It may be that our future will lay upon us more than one stern test. Our past will have taught us how to meet it unshaken. For the present, the work to which we are all equally bound is to arrive at a reasoned tranquillity within our borders; to regain prosperity without self-seeking; and to carry with us those whom the burden of past years has disheartened or overborne.

My life's aim has been to serve as I might, towards those ends. Your loyalty, your confidence in me has been my abundant reward.

I speak now from my home and from my heart to you all. To men and women so cut off by the snows, the desert, or the sea, that only voices out of the air can reach them: to those cut off from fuller life by blindness, sickness, or infirmity; and to those who are celebrating this day with their children and grand-children. To all – to each – I wish a Happy Christmas. God Bless you!

GEORGE VI – RELUCTANT BROADCASTER

There was no royal broadcast at Christmas 1936 – the nation was stunned by the abdication of Edward VIII and the succession of his brother the Duke of York, a shy and self-effacing man who was most reluctant to take on his mantle. In the event, the new King saw his country through one of the most difficult times in its history.

The first Christmas Day of King George VI's reign fell exactly a fortnight after his predecessor's farewell broadcast and departure for France. The new monarch was still in a state of shock. Nor did he feel ready so soon, or perhaps ever, to take his father's place on a broadcasting occasion which the old King had, in three short years, so uniquely made his own. He had another anxiety, which in the past had sometimes come near to overwhelming him. Since the age of 7, he had suffered from a speech impediment which was most pronounced when he was excited or nervous. Within the family circle, it all but disappeared. (There have been suggestions that the stammer may have originated at the time when, as a left-handed child, he was forced to use his right hand for writing and other active pursuits) . . .

On Christmas Day 1939, the first Christmas of the war, The King decided that he must speak 'live' again to his peoples throughout the world. At the beginning of the reign, the Prime Minister, Neville Chamberlain, had expressed the opinion that annual broadcasts by the sovereign were not desirable. There would not be sufficiently varied or important things to say, and the Crown might consequently be devalued. But now there *were* important things to be said to a people fighting against great odds to preserve their own kind of freedom; things that spoke of the sheer endurability of the human spirit.

Each Christmas, even in the early days against a seemingly infinite catalogue of disasters, The King spoke of his unswerving faith in the ultimate survival of his island people, and what he came more and more to call the free 'Commonwealth of Nations'. He talked often out of his own personal experience. He sent a message to the navy from 'the senior officers to the last boy who has joined up', and at once was revealed the timid midshipman who had seen service in the Battle of Jutland. 'This time we are all in the front line,' he said, and everyone remembered that weeks before, a stick of six bombs had straddled his own London home. It was not only those on the Home Front who listened eagerly to the broadcasts. In 1942, on Christmas Day, men of the Eighth Army in North Africa listened in tanks, trucks, and temporary dug-outs in the sand-dunes, or in silent circles under the dismal sky. A war correspondent noted, 'Some were wearing battledress, some British warms, some sheepskin coats, and all gathered near the fire which had been made in a petrol tin beside a Sherman tank. Next to me was a Czech officer who fought in Poland against the Germans. On the other side was a South African Sapper with two New Zealanders and a Scottish Sergeant. No word was spoken until the speech was ended, and then as "God Save The King" was played everyone came to attention, and the officers saluted. I noticed the suspicion of tears in the eyes of more than one man . . .' To 'the roar of the lion' as Churchill's splendid wartime speeches have been called, was added the gentler but equally stirring and resolute voice of the King.

From *Voices out of the Air* by Tom Fleming

King George VI ended his 1939 broadcast with words from the poem 'The Gate of the Year' by Minnie Louise Haskins. After his death in 1952 these same words were inscribed on the gates of the Memorial Chapel at Windsor Castle, where he is buried.

A new year is at hand. We cannot tell what it will bring. If it brings peace, how thankful we shall all be. If it brings us continued struggle we shall remain undaunted. In the meantime I feel that we may all find a message of encouragement in the lines which, in my closing words, I would like to say to you: – 'I said to the man who stood at the Gate of the Year, "Give me a light that I may tread safely into the unknown." And he replied, "Go out into the darkness, and put your hand into the Hand of God. That shall be to you better than light, and safer than a known way."'

May that Almighty Hand guide and uphold us all.

ELIZABETH II – '*ANNUS HORRIBILIS*'

Queen Elizabeth made her first Christmas broadcast in 1952. The following year she was in New Zealand at Christmastime and spoke from Auckland. Four years later the message was seen on

television for the first time. Perhaps the most memorable broadcast
of her reign to date is that of 1992, a year that saw recession and
unemployment at home, changing relationships with Europe and
the Commonwealth overseas, and within the Queen's own family.
The marriages of Prince Charles and Prince Andrew broke up,
while Princess Anne remarried. Then the year ended with a
devastating fire in the state rooms of Windsor Castle, her favourite
home. In her Christmas broadcast she referred to the year as an
'annus horribilis'.

1992 is not a year I shall look back on with undiluted
pleasure. In the words of one of my more sympathetic
correspondents, it has turned out to be an *annus*
horribilis.

I sometimes wonder how future generations will judge
the events of this tumultuous year. I dare say that
history will take a slightly more moderate view than
some contemporary commentators. Distance is well
known to lend enchantment, even to the less attractive
views.

After all, it has the inestimable value of hindsight. But
it can also lend an extra dimension to judgement, giving
it a leavening of moderation and compassion – even of
wisdom – that is sometimes lacking in the reactions of
those whose task it is in life to offer instant opinions on
all things great and small. No section of the community
has all the virtues, nor does it have all the vices. I am
quite sure that most people try to do their jobs as best
they can, even if the result is not always entirely

successful. He who has never failed to reach perfection has a right to be the harshest critic.

There can be no doubt, of course, that criticism is good for people and institutions that are a part of public life. No institution – City, monarchy, whatever – should expect to be free from scrutiny of those who give their loyalty and support, not to mention those who don't.

But we are all part of the same fabric of our national society and that scrutiny, by one part of another, can be just as effective if it is made with a touch of gentleness, good humour and understanding.

This sort of questioning can also act, and so it should do, as an effective agent of change.

Dickens with Cartier at Sandringham

The Duke of Windsor, Giles St Aubyn and Georgina Battiscombe

Unlike their predecessors twentieth-century kings, queens and princes did not have to spend Christmas in draughty castles holding nobles, serfs and bitter cold at bay; festive days could now be enjoyed at home with their family. Sandringham was Edward VII's favourite home, and is loved to the present day by his descendants because it is not a great castle but a country house where they can enjoy privacy.

To the young Prince of Wales, later King Edward VIII, the place was magical.

Christmas at Sandringham was Dickens in a Cartier setting. It was more of a family gathering, and my grandparents always came back for that. Since serious purpose was usually injected even into our pleasures, Mr. Hansell, working to instil in us a knowledge of the ancient meanings of this Christmas fête, would attempt to explain to us the religious meaning of the Nativity. He also read to us Dickens's well-known Christmas story; and Mama, with her lady-in-waiting at the piano, taught us the Christmas carols. And to remind us to think of others, my parents always took us on Christmas Eve to the coach-house at the stables to watch the distribution of meat to the employees on the estate. When, from these days of rationing and controls, I look back upon this simple scene, I appreciate, as I did not then, the bounty thus displayed. Inside the coach-house, on long tables covered with white tablecloths were laid scores of bloody joints of beef, one for each family, and each tagged with the name of the recipient. Outside in the stable yard, waiting their turn, were the gamekeepers, gardeners, foresters, and stable hands, or their wives – in all some three hundred people. My grandparents with their family sat just inside near the door of the coach-house; and, as the employees walked out with their meat, the men touching their caps and the women

Sandringham House, Norfolk. This was King Edward VII's chosen residence during the Christmas holiday. It remained a family favourite throughout the twentieth century.

making a quick bob of a curtsey, the King wished each a Happy Christmas.

In my family the display of the Christmas tree and the exchange of gifts always took place on Christmas Eve. After tea we all piled into my father's omnibus, ordinarily used for transporting the servants, and rode up to the Big House, where my grandparents would be waiting in the Saloon with some of the older members of the Household, who usually spent Christmas with them. It would not be long before the loud banging of a gong heralded the approach of Santa Claus himself. An instant later there would appear in our midst the real thing: a tall, hooded figure in full regalia, a flowing white beard, red coat, black patent-leather boots, and over his shoulder a bulging bag. The fact that we knew this resplendent impersonator to be one of the upper servants in no way diminished our joy over his arrival. After bowing to the King and Queen, who would greet him jovially, Santa Claus led the company out of the Saloon towards the Ballroom. The double doors flew open before his advance, revealing in the centre of the room a fir-tree from the woods, tall enough to touch the ceiling, festooned with tinsel, tinted glass balls, patches of cotton-wool in imitation of snow, and ablaze with candles. But, as with everything else at Sandringham, even the business of Christmas proceeded along prescribed lines. Around the Ballroom were tables heaped with presents, with an ample section marked off for each person, the first for the King and the Queen, the next for my mother and father, and the rest more or less according to precedence.

The children's tables were in a far corner, segregated from the rest. This precaution was no doubt intended to safeguard a precious Fabergé jade masterpiece or a bejewelled clock on my grandmother's table from becoming the casualty of a wild shot from a toy gun or a misdirected football issuing from our direction. We children were always shown our presents last, and the suspense was agonizing. And when finally our turn came, the Ballroom floor was rapidly inundated with a sea of

A letter written by the Prince of Wales on Christmas Day, 1919. This letter illustrates not only the pressures he felt even before he became King, but also the marked contrast between this Christmas and the many happy holidays he had spent at Sandringham over the festive period earlier in his life.

wrapping-paper, through which we pedalled and honked in toy motors.

On the way home we might pass the village choir with its winking lanterns on its way to sing Christmas carols to the King and Queen.

From *A King's Story* by the Duke of Windsor

Even queens could let their hair down at Christmas – without the slightest loss of royal dignity of course. Here is the 'Big House', as they called the main Sandringham mansion, under the Prince of Wales (later Edward VII).

Sandringham was famous for its practical jokes: for some they were one of its terrors, for others part of its charm. It was thought tremendously funny when a wretched midshipman devoured a mince-pie made of mustard, or when a live lobster was hidden in somebody's bed. Alix [Princess of Wales] was less disposed to indulge in practical jokes than to encourage rough-and-tumble games, such as tobogganing downstairs on a silver tray. Mary Bulteel, who married Henry Ponsonby, regarded the royal sense of humour with undisguised contempt. Prince Albert, she said, would go into 'fits of laughter at anything like a practical joke; for instance, if anyone caught his foot in a mat, or nearly fell into the fire or out of a window, the mirth of the whole Royal Family knew no bounds'. Lord Granville used to say that he never bothered to tell his best stories at Court, 'when pretending to pinch one's finger in a door would answer better'.

From *Edward VII: Prince and King* by Giles St Aubyn

Alexandra's sense of humour may hardly have gone far beyond
tobogganing downstairs on silver teatrays, and only some of her
household enjoyed it.

She was nothing of an intellectual; 'the melancholy thing
is that neither he [the Prince of Wales] nor the darling
Princess ever care to open a book', lamented Lady
Frederick Cavendish, unconsciously echoing a complaint
frequently made by Queen Victoria. When other people
opened a book in her presence the result could be
surprising. At her first meeting with Tennyson she
politely asked him to read aloud the famous *Ode of
Welcome* which he had written for her wedding.
Halfway through, the situation struck them both as
unbearably funny; the book fell on the floor and
Princess and poet went into fits of uncontrollable
laughter.

This sense of fun – it can hardly be described as a full-
blown sense of humour – went hand in hand with a
liking, in which her husband shared, for practical jokes
and for rough-and-tumble horse-play. In their letters she
and her son Prince George would recall with sentimental
pleasure the way in which they had squirted each other
with soda-water syphons during the Christmas festivities
at Sandringham. The Princess could squirt and be
squirted and yet keep her dignity. . . . Likewise at
bedtime, high jinks with all the ladies in the corridors,
and yet through it all one had a sense of perfect womanly
dignity and a certainty that one could never go an inch

too far with her. She can gather up her beautiful bright stateliness at any moment.

This cheerful informal spirit was characteristic of Sandringham parties. 'It is very jolly here indeed,' wrote Oliver Montagu's brother Victor, 'very unstiff and only a certain amount of etiquette, very quiet and gentleman-like altogether.' . . . There would be sport of all kinds to entertain the guests, hunting as well as shooting, and in very hard weather, games of ice-hockey, and skating on the lake, a sport in which the Princess delighted in spite of her lame leg. She was more interested than ever in horses and when wishing to buy or sell she would consult Henry Chaplin, one of her husband's more intimate friends and a famous judge of horse-flesh. To dogs she was almost ludicrously devoted, first pugs and later 'Japanese spaniels' and pekinese being her favourite breeds. She also cherished a liking for parrots – a white cockatoo lived permanently in the hall at Sandringham – although even she admitted to feeling daunted when a friend presented her with no less than forty of these birds.

From *Queen Alexandra* by Georgina Battiscombe, published by Constable

By the 1950s a new generation of the royal house was at Sandringham for Christmas. Princess Elizabeth had married in 1947 and Prince Charles was born the following year to brighten the last years of the life of his grandfather, King George VI.

Prince Charles was taken there for Christmas when five weeks old. His mother suffered the wry experience of an attack of measles which confined her to her room and separated her from her baby. Prince Charles was again in the care of his grandparents at Sandringham for Christmas, 1950, when Princess Elizabeth had joined Prince Philip in Malta. 'He is too sweet stumping around the room,' the King wrote fondly to his daughter. 'We shall love having him at Sandringham. He is the fifth generation to live there and I hope he will get to love the place.'

From *Sandringham, The Story of a Royal House*
by Helen Cathcart

Love Spoils the Fun

The Duke of Windsor and Dina Wells Hood

Christmas 1935 at Sandringham was difficult. The health of the elderly George V was failing and the Prince of Wales had too much on his mind to relax. He knew he would be called on soon to succeed to the throne – but uppermost in the Prince's mind was that he had fallen in love with an American divorcée, Wallis Simpson, and it was far from certain that she would be accepted by the British people.

Princess Margaret and Princess Elizabeth in a scene from the pantomime
Cinderella, 1941. The royal family enthusiastically made their own festive
entertainment during the difficult years of the Second World War.

A few days later I was at Sandringham for the family
Christmas gathering. My brothers and their wives were
already there. My father had grown thin and bent; we
all shared a sense of foreboding that this might well be
his last Christmas; so we tried to make it an especially

happy one. In the spacious white ballroom of the Big House, where we had all had such fun in my grandfather's time, a fourth generation had begun to assert itself. Bertie's two children, Elizabeth, who was then nine, and her sister, Margaret Rose, romped around the twenty-foot tree. Yet, in this closely knit fabric of family ties I felt detached and lonely. My brothers were secure in their private lives; whereas I was caught up in an inner conflict and would have no peace of mind until I had resolved it. But again this was hardly the time or the place. My father died before another opportunity presented itself.

From *A King's Story* by the Duke of Windsor

After his abdication in 1936, King Edward VIII, now the Duke of Windsor, and Wallis Simpson, whom he had married, lived in France. They decided to spend Christmas 1938 with a small group of friends at the Château La Croë, which they rented at Antibes. The Duke's private secretary Dina Wells Hood helped to organise the festivities.

One evening early in December I received a long-distance call from one of the leading evening papers in London asking for confirmation of a story which had appeared earlier in the day as front page news in another paper. The story was to the effect that the Duke and Duchess had invited a British working man with his wife and two children to spend Christmas with them at their Riviera home La Croë. The article stated that the whole family had accepted; that the Duke had issued his invitation because he was 'anxious to spend the holiday in the company of one of the ordinary people of his country'. The Duchess was said to be looking forward to giving the children a party and a Christmas tree. There was no truth at all in the story and I said so, but this did not end the matter. Some half dozen more newspapers put through long-distance calls that night and the next day, asking the same question.

When I reported this yarn to the Duke, his comment was, 'A British workman would be the last person to appreciate such an invitation. It would only make him thoroughly uncomfortable.' For the next ten days questions about this story kept cropping up . . .

On Christmas morning, which was fine and sunny, the Duke and Duchess attended the service at the little English church on the road to Antibes. Being the parish church of La Croë, they made a point of supporting it both by subscriptions and by occasional attendances. Among the Christmas cheques there was always one for the local padre.

After Church the whole household assembled in the big lounge. The house party came too and a few guests from the neighbourhood. The great silver and white Christmas tree standing by the terrace windows was visible from end to end of the Château and its glittering branches were reflected back and forth in the tall mirrored panelling of the room. . . . La Croë that morning had more than ever the air of a large English country house. The Christmas morning ceremony added a touch of friendly old-world feudalism to the scene.

The servants filed up one after the other to receive their gifts, bowing or curtseying to Their Royal Highnesses. Standing beside the great white tree, the Duke and Duchess smilingly handed out the presents. . . . The Duchess herself had chosen and wrapped up all the gifts, not only for her guests but for each member of her staff as well. She presented me with a very lovely set of beauty preparations.

From *Working for the Windsors* by Dina Wells Hood

Fun and James

Joan Aiken

Joan Aiken's children's books are a rich blend of all the ingredients a young person loves in a story – fantasy, adventure, kidnapping, wild animals, danger and a happy ending.

In Black Hearts in Battersea *history's tables have been turned: King James III is on the throne and Hanoverian George is the Pretender. After many adventures the heroes Simon and Sophie help to rescue King Jamie from the Duke of Battersea's castle, where he is trapped by the wicked Buckle and Mr and*

Mrs Twite. There is a happy ending to this outrageous royal Christmas tale.

'Is my coronet on straight, Sophie? Are my gloves properly buttoned? These diamond buttons stick so –'

'Come on, come on, Hettie, there's no time to waste. I can hear the cheers! His Majesty will be here at any moment!'

The Duke [of Battersea] took his wife's arm and fairly ran her down the stairs . . . As they descended, Buckle's voice could be heard below, giving orders to a large number of people.

'You all know what you have to do – every soul to be out at half past eight. After the fanfare and the dinner – disperse! Each carry something – Midwink take charge of the jewels – Scrimshaw the plate –'

'Good evening, Mr Buckle,' The Duke said. 'Are the arrangements for His Majesty's reception all complete?'

Buckle whipped round. For an instant an ugly expression came over his face, but this was rapidly replaced by his usual pale-eyed impassive stare.

'Quite ready, your Graces,' he replied smoothly. 'I am glad to welcome your Graces back to Battersea.'

'Well you won't be when you hear our news!' the Duke snapped. 'We know that you're a damned scoundrel, who palmed off your own whey-faced brat in place of my nephew and niece, and tried to murder me three times! But your crimes have caught up with you, and I shall be surprised if you don't end your days in the Tower, you rogue! The Bow Street men and the

Yeomanry are on their way now; we don't want any unpleasant scenes at present, but as soon as His Majesty has left you'll be arrested.'

Mr Buckle's eyes flashed but he replied in a low, even tone:

'Your Grace is mistaken. I intend to amend my ways. I see my faults – I am truly sorry – and in future your Grace will have nothing to complain of.'

'Well,' said the Duke, a little mollified, 'if you are *truly* sorry –'

'William!' exclaimed the scandalized Duchess. 'Don't believe a word the hypocrite says! I am sure he has not the least intention –'

'Hark!' interposed Sophie. 'Here is His Majesty! I can hear the fanfare, and the students cheering.'

Indeed, as the Royal sleigh left the

frozen Thames, along which it had sped from Hampton Court, and crossed the short snowy stretch of park to the Castle, the assembled students burst into loyal shouts:

'Hooray for Jamie Three!'

'Long live King Jim, good luck to him!'

'Yoicks, your Majesty!'

The Duke and Duchess, with Sophie behind them, ran

down the red-carpeted front steps of the Castle to greet His Majesty, while the students formed a ring and, with snowballs and horse-chestnuts, kept the inquisitive wolves from coming too close.

'Sire, this is a happy day. We are so pleased to welcome you to our humble roof –'

'Och, weel, noo, Battersea, it's nice to hear that. And how's your gude lady?'

The King was a little, dapper, elderly Scottish gentleman, plainly dressed in black, with a shovel hat on top of his snuff-coloured wig. He carried a slender hooked cane, and a large black bird perched on his wrist, which, at sight of the duchess, opened its beak and gravely remarked:

'What's your wull, my bonny hinny?'

'Mercy on us!' exclaimed her Grace. 'Where did your Majesty get that heathen bird?'

'Why, ma'am, the Sultan of Zanzibar gave her to me for a Christmas present. And I find her a great convenience – don't I, Jeannie, my lass? – for there's a wheen Hanoverians aye trying to slip a wee drop of poison into my victuals, so I e'en employ Jeannie as a taster. She takes a nip of brose and a nibble of parritch, and soon has the poisoned meat sorted. Not that I mean to decry your hospitality, ma'am, but one must be careful.'

'Why yes, yes indeed one must!' The flustered Duchess then pulled herself together and graciously invited His Majesty to do himself the trouble of stepping into the banqueting-hall. Sophie, following, noticed a pale gleam in Buckle's eyes, and thought he looked as if he meant mischief.

'Will you have a mince-pie, Your Majesty?'

'Na, na, thank you, Duchess. They play the very deuce with my digestion. But Jeannie will, won't you, lass?'

Jeannie ate several mince-pies with every appearance of satisfaction, smacking her beak over the prune brandy.

'Are they safe?' Dr Field whispered to Sophie.

'I brought them from Chippings,' she whispered back.

'I wouldn't trust the mince-pies Mr Buckle had provided.'

Even so, none of the party save Jeannie felt inclined to sample the mince-pies. She, after her fourth, perhaps because of the prune brandy, suddenly became over-excited, flew round the banqueting-hall twice, pecked Mr Buckle on the ear, and disappeared through a small open window.

'Jeannie – come back, lass!' cried her master, starting up. 'A gold guinea to the man who catches her!'

None of the footmen seemed moved by this appeal; they stood motionless, and one or two of them sniggered. Sophie felt ready to sink with shame, but Dr Field went to the window and shouted to the students outside:

'His Majesty offers a gold guinea to the person who brings back his pet bird.'

A tremendous cheer went up, and the sound of many running feet could be heard, accompanied by cries of hope and disappointment.

'Shall we adjourn to the library for coffee?' the Duke suggested. 'I believe later on we are to see some fireworks.' The party began moving up the stairs. 'I daresay one of the students will soon bring back your bird –' the Duke was going on comfortably, when suddenly the most astonishing hubbub – shouts, shots, and crashes – broke out downstairs by the main doors.

'Gracious heavens!' cried the Duchess in alarm. 'What can be going on!'

A somewhat bedraggled Gus burst through the Castle doors and came charging up the stairs. His hair stood on end, one eye was blacked, and his face was covered by what looked like peck-marks, but he held the squawking Jeannie triumphantly in both hands.

'Here you are, Your Majesty!' he panted. 'And I wish you joy of her! She's a Tartar! But sir and ma'am and Your Majesty, I don't think you should stay here, I don't indeed. Those villains downstairs are up to tricks, I believe. I had the devil's own job to get in, they were all massed about the hall with pikes and Pictclobbers. The sooner you are all out of the Castle, the better it will be, in my opinion.'

'Oh dear, oh, William!' lamented the Duchess. 'We should never have let His Majesty come here –'

'Nonsense, Hettie. The Yeomanry will be here directly. All we need do is keep calm and retire to the library till it all blows over.'

'Let us go higher up! That noise terrifies me – it sounds as if they are all fighting each other before coming up to murder us.'

'What does His Majesty say?'

His Majesty had been busy settling Jeannie's ruffled plumes and politely affecting to be unaware of his hosts' problems. Appealed to, he said amiably:

'Och, let us go higher up, by all means. Did ye not say there were to be fireworks? The higher up, the better the view.'

'I winna say nay to a wee dram,' remarked Jeannie unexpectedly.

'Hush, ye ill-mannered bird. Lead the way upstairs, then, Battersea.'

The Duke had the key to a small privy staircase leading to the battlements, and up this he led the King, while the rest of the party followed.

It was now almost dark, except for a fiery pink streak lying across the western sky: down below in the park the obscurity was broken by flashes as the students skirmished with the wolves and aimed a shot from time to time at Hanoverians in the Castle doorway.

'Brave boys! They're keeping the scoundrels boxed in!' exclaimed the Duke. 'When the Yeomanry come – oh why *don't* they come?'

'But look – look who *is* coming!' Sophie pointed, almost stammering in her excitement. 'The balloon! It must be Simon!'

An applauding shout went up from the students as the balloon drifted over them, shining in the light of the gas flambeaux which were now beginning to illuminate the park. Simon leaned over the side and shouted down urgently:

'Keep away from the Castle! Away, for your lives!'

Then he threw out some ballast, and the balloon soared up to the level of the battlements. Grasping the hooked end of the King's cane, he was drawn close to the Castle walls.

'Please, your Graces and Your Majesty – don't waste a minute!' he begged. 'Climb on board, quick! You are in the most deadly danger – there is not an instant to be lost!'

With the Hanoverians furiously trying to bring down King Jamie's balloon there were more adventures before he landed safely but his journey was brought to a happy conclusion, although the poor old Duke of Battersea's castle suffered much damage.

. . . 'Dod!' said King James. 'Nae wonder ye were in sich a hurry, my lad! We're obleeged to ye – very. Aweel, aweel, that rids the world of a muckle nest of Hanoverians – but I'm afeered there's no' much left of your Castle, Battersea.'

'No matter, no matter!' said the Duke somewhat distractedly. 'To tell truth, I never greatly cared for it. I should prefer to live at Chippings. We'll lay out a pleasure-garden on the site – yes, that will be much better. Simon, my dear boy, I can't thank you sufficiently. we are indebted to you for all our lives. Sire, may I present to you my nephew Simon, Lord Bakerloo. As for those miserable Yeomanry and Bow Street Runners, we might well never have applied to them for all the help they have been . . .'

'But as they sank slowly towards the snowy grounds of the Academy, a sound of martial music was heard: the banging of drums and squealing of fifes heralded the arrival of the Chelsea Yeomanry, who came marching in brave array down the Chelsea Bridge Road, while along the bank of the river twenty Bow Street Officers galloped at full speed, led by Mr Cobb. Meanwhile, the students, having observed the balloon's escape, had come running across the park, and all these forces converged to welcome the rescued party as they reached the ground.

Luckily, perhaps, at this moment the Royal sleigh . . . arrived at the river-bank with its attendant outriders. The King and his guests were all packed in, under layers of swansdown rugs. Goodbyes were shouted, whips were cracked.

'I'll be back in the morning early . . . !' Simon shouted.

'And give a Christmas dinner to thank everybody for their help!' shouted the Duke.

. . . The sleigh-bells jingled, the horses began to move away in their felt slippers.

'Good night! Merry Christmas! God Save King James!'

'Merry Christmas!'

'And a Happy New Year!'

Faster and faster the procession glided off into the dark, a long trail of brilliant lights, red, gold and blue, winding along the frozen Thames to Hampton Court, until at last the glitter and the music of the bells died away, and the students went home to bed, and the mysterious peace of Christmas night descended once again on Battersea Park.

Bibliographic Sources

Aiken, Joan. *Black Hearts in Battersea*, London, Red Fox, 1992 (the extract reproduced here is used by permission of the Random House Group Limited)

Aitchison, Nick. *Scotland's Stone of Destiny*, Stroud, Tempus, 2000

The Anglo-Saxon Chronicle, London, Everyman edn, 1912

Battiscombe, Georgina. *Queen Alexandra*, London, Constable, 1969

Benson, A.C. and Esher, Viscount (eds). *The Letters of Queen Victoria*, London, John Murray, 1907

Blind Harry (Harry the Minstrel). *Wallace*, translated by William Hamilton of Gilbertfield, 1722; National Library of Scotland

Buckle, G.E. (ed.). *The Letters of Queen Victoria, Third Series 1886–1901*, London, John Murray, 1930–2

Cathcart, Helen. *Sandringham, The Story of a Royal House*, London, W.H. Allen, 1964

Craig, Elizabeth. *The English Royal Cookbook*, New York, Hippocrene Books, 1998

Dearmer, P., Vaughan Williams, R. and Shaw, M. *The Oxford Book of Carols*, London, OUP, 1928

A Diary of Royal Movements and of Personal Events and Incidents in the Life and Reign of HM Queen Victoria, 1883

Dickens, Charles. *The Life of Our Lord*, London, Associated Newspapers, 1934

Douglas, Hugh. *The Hogmanay Companion*, Glasgow, Neil Wilson Publishing, 1993

Douglas, Hugh. *The Private Passions of Bonnie Prince Charlie*, Stroud, Sutton Publishing, 1995

Dunnett, Dorothy. *To Lie with Lions*, London, Michael Joseph, 1995; New York, Alfred A. Knopf (division of Random House), 1996

Eliot, T.S. *Murder in the Cathedral*, London, Faber & Faber, 1935

Evelyn, John. *Diary*, 1653–88

Fleming, Tom. *Voices Out of the Air*, London, Heinemann, 1981 (the extracts reproduced here are used by permission of the Random House Group Limited)

George, Margaret. *The Autobiography of Henry VIII*, New York, St Martin's Press, 1986; London, Macmillan, 1988

Henisch, Bridget Ann. *Cakes and Characters*, London & Totnes, Prospect Books, 1984

Hibbert, Christopher (ed.). *Queen Victoria in her Letters and Journals*, Stroud, Sutton Publishing, 2000

Hilliam, David. *Monarchs, Murders and Mistresses*, Stroud, Sutton Publishing, 2000

The History and Antiquities of the City of York, York, 1785

Hotson, Leslie. *The First Night of Twelfth Night*, London, Rupert Hart-Davis, 1954

Longford, Elizabeth. *Victoria R.I.*, London, Weidenfeld & Nicolson, 1964

Macleod, John. *Dynasty – The Stuarts 1560–1807*, London, Hodder & Stoughton, 1999

The Paston Letters: A Selection in Modern Spelling, edited with an Introduction by Norman Davies, Oxford, Oxford World's Classics, Oxford University Press, 1999

Pepys, Samuel. *Diary*, 1660–3

Rowell, George. *Queen Victoria Goes to the Theatre*, London, Paul Elek, 1978

St Aubyn, Giles. *Edward VII: Prince and King*, London, Collins, 1979

Schama, Simon. *A History of Britain, Vol. 1 3000 BC–AD 1603*, London, BBC Worldwide, 2000

Scheele, Godfrey and Margaret. *The Prince Consort: Man of Many Facets*, London, Allan Wingate, 1977

Wells Hood, Dina. *Working for the Windsors*, Allan Wingate, 1957

Windsor, the Duke of. *A King's Story*, London, Prion Books, 1998

Wyndham-Lewis, D.B. and Hesseltine, G.C. *A Christmas Book; An Anthology for Moderns*, London, J.M. Dent, 1928 (by permission of The Orion Publishing Group)